Cognitive Systems Monographs

Volume 5

Editors: Rüdiger Dillmann · Yoshihiko Nakamura · Stefan Schaal · David Vernon

T0180915

Cognitive Systems Monographs

Volume 8

Edilson de Aguiar

Animation and
Performance Capture
Using Digitized Models

 Springer

Rüdiger Dillmann, University of Karlsruhe, Faculty of Informatics, Institute of Anthropomatics, Humanoids and Intelligence Systems Laboratories, Kaiserstr. 12, 76131 Karlsruhe, Germany

Yoshihiko Nakamura, Tokyo University Fac. Engineering, Dept. Mechano-Informatics, 7-3-1 Hongo, Bukyo-ku Tokyo, 113-8656, Japan

Stefan Schaal, University of Southern California, Department Computer Science, Computational Learning & Motor Control Lab., Los Angeles, CA 90089-2905, USA

David Vernon, Khalifa University Department of Computer Engineering, PO Box 573, Sharjah, United Arab Emirates

Author

Dr.-Ing. Edilson de Aguiar
Carnegie Mellon University
Disney Reseach Pittsburgh
4615 Forbes Avenue
Pittsburg, PA 15213
USA
E-mail: edilson@disneyresearch.com

ISBN 978-3-642-26189-3   e-ISBN 978-3-642-10316-2

DOI 10.1007/978-3-642-10316-2

Cognitive Systems Monographs   ISSN 1867-4925

Typeset & Cover Design: Scientific Publishing Services Pvt. Ltd., Chennai, India.

Printed in acid-free paper

5 4 3 2 1 0

springer.com

To
Aparicio de Aguiar
and
Maria Auxiliadora de Aguiar

Foreword

Vision is our strongest sense. It enables us to quickly perceive and analyze our surroundings such that we can find our way around, recognize people and places, and avoid potential dangers. However, this rather functional way of looking at the human visual sense only grasps a fraction of the rich variety of sensual experiences that are channeled through optical stimuli. Visual perception is not only a tool for us but it can also induce great emotions, for instance if we are looking at a painting we like, or when we are intrigued by the visual effects of a feature film. The field of computer science that aims at algorithmically modeling these aspects of the human visual system is called visual computing. The field of visual computing subdivides in several more specific research areas, and i will briefly look at two of them in the following.

Researchers in computer vision and artificial intelligence are trying to equip computers and autonomous systems with visual analysis capabilities that match the ones of real humans. In recent years, this area of research has seen tremendous progress. Computers can nowadays perform optical recognition tasks, objects or people in image sequences can be tracked, and optical scene analysis can provide control inputs to steer autonomous vehicles. However, if we compare the performance, robustness and application range of even the best computer vision system today to the abilities of the human visual system, we have to humbly conclude that the field of computer vision is still in its infancy.

While computer vision focuses on the functional or reconstruction side of visual computing, computer graphics focuses on the synthesis or display aspect. In recent years algorithms for creating photo-realistic virtual imagery have greatly improved. Nowadays we can simulate entire virtual cities or imaginary foreign planets at a high visual fidelity, albeit at very high computational cost. Unfortunately, the same claim cannot be made for the rendering of virtual humans or virtual actors. Over millions of years the human visual system has developed the ability to quickly assess other humans, and it thus unmasks in a glimpse of an eye even the slightest flaw in the appearance of a virtual actor. It is therefore of utmost importance that all aspects of a virtual human, including appearance and lighting effects at the surface, geometry and motion are modeled at the highest possible level of detail. It is no wonder that achieving such a high level of quality comes at a high prices which can be measured in several man months of work for animators.

Animation professionals can resort to a set of acquisition tools which help them to measure certain aspects of a virtual human, e.g. his motion or his shape from real world subjects. Laser triangulation scanners can acquire full-body geometry in a static pose. Marker-based motion capture systems can be employed to measure skeletal motion parameters, but are often cumbersome to use since they require the captured subject to wear optical markings on the body. Recently, in the field of computer vision we have also seen marker-less capturing systems which do not require such optical beacons and only expect multi-view video of an actor as input. However, most of these systems do not capture more than skeletal motion, require controlled recording conditions, and fail to reconstruct actors in normal everyday clothing (e.g. a skirt). It is thus fair to conclude that even state-of-the-art measurement technology only captures a small subset of the complexity of a moving human's appearance. Ideally, one would want to unify the process and measure much richer performance models, i.e representations of detailed time-varying geometry and appearance using just one set of multi-view video recordings.

This book presents such joint reconstruction and display approaches that enable easier capturing of more complete scene models, as well as more faithful rendering of virtual humans. It describes a variety of significant leaps forward which the fields of human performance capture and animation have recently seen. In my opinion the book takes a refreshingly different perspective on cognitive system modeling in general and visual computing in particular. It does not focus on only the vision or graphics side but convincingly demonstrates that a joint investigation of both facets enables significant technological progress. I am convinced that also in other fields of computer science and cognitive system modeling such a more integrated approach to solving hard problems will proof highly successful.

Saarbruecken, Germany
September 2009

Christian Theobalt
MPI Informatik

Preface

In computer graphics, it is still challenging to authentically create virtual doubles of real-world actors. Although the interplay of all steps required by the traditional skeleton-based animation pipeline delivers realistic animations, the whole process is still very time-consuming. Current motion capture methods are not able to capture the time-varying dynamic geometry of the moving actors and need to be integrated with other special acquisition techniques. Furthermore, dealing with subjects wearing arbitrary apparel is still not possible. Another problem is that, even if it was possible to capture mesh animations, it would still be difficult to post-process or modify them. Not many papers in the literature have looked into this problem so far.

In this book, we propose algorithms to solve these problems: first, we describe two efficient techniques to simplify the overall animation process. Afterwards, we detail three algorithmic solutions to capture a spatio-temporally coherent dynamic scene representation even from subjects wearing loose and arbitrary everyday apparel. At the end, we also propose two novel algorithms to process mesh animations. By this means, real-world sequences can be accurately captured and transformed into fully-rigged virtual characters and become amenable to higher-level animation creation, e.g. by applying non-photorealistic rendering styles.

This book consists of four parts:

- Part I begins with the description of some general theoretical background information and elementary techniques shared by many projects in this book. Thereafter, the studio used to acquire the input data for the projects described in this book is presented.
- Part II reviews the steps involved in the traditional skeleton-based character animation paradigm and proposes two mesh-based alternatives to simplify the overhead of the conventional process. Both techniques can be directly integrated in the traditional pipeline and are able to generate character animations with realistic body deformations, as well as transfer motions between different subjects.
- Part III describes three algorithmic variants to passively capture the performance of human actors using a deformable model as underlying scene representation from multiple video streams. The algorithms jointly reconstruct spatio-temporally

coherent time-varying geometry, motion, and textural surface appearance even from subjects wearing everyday apparel, which is still challenging for related marker-based or marker-free systems. By using the acquired high-quality scene representations, we also developed a system to generate realistic 3D Videos.

- Part IV proposes two novel techniques to simplify the processing of mesh animations. First, an automatic method to bridge the gap between the mesh-based and the skeletal paradigms is presented. Thereafter, a method to automatically transform mesh animations into animation collages, a new non-photorealistic rendering style for animations, is proposed.

Although the methods described in this book are usually tailored to deal with human actors, their fundamental principles can also be applied to a larger class of subjects. Each method described here can be regarded as a solution to a particular problem or used as a building block for a larger application. All together, they exceed the capabilities of many related capture techniques and form a powerful system to accurately capture, manipulate, and realistically render real-world human performances.

Pittsburgh, PA
September 2009   Edilson de Aguiar

Acknowledgements

This book is adapted from my PhD dissertation and it would not have been possible without the help and support of many people. First of all, I would like to thank my supervisors Prof. Dr. Hans-Peter Seidel and Prof. Dr. Christian Theobalt. Prof. Seidel gave me the opportunity to work in an excellent and inspiring environment as the Max-Planck-Institut für Informatik (MPI) and supported me pursuing my own research interests.

I am also grateful to Prof. Theobalt, who always had time to discuss ongoing and future projects. I also thank him for the invaluable scientific guidance in my research. He has been working with me since the beginning of my PhD and we worked together on all projects described in this book.

Furthermore, I would like to thank Prof. Dr. Marcus Magnor for being my senior supervisor during the beginning of my PhD, Prof. Dr. Sebastian Thrun for hosting me in Stanford during my exchange research visit, and Prof. Dr. Jessica K. Hodgins who have agreed to be part of my graduation committee.

Special thanks go to all my former colleagues in the Computer Graphics Group at the MPI. Their cooperation, competence, creativity, and steady motivation makes the MPI the special place it is. In particular, I owe thanks to Naveed Ahmed, Christian Rössl, Carsten Stoll and Rhaleb Zayer, who were co-authors on some of my papers, Hitoshi Yamauchi for the support with the geometric modeling library, Andreas Pomi for helping with the studio.

I also thank Mayra Castro for the support during the production of this book and the people who kindly allowed me to record and scan them for my research and to many colleagues at the MPI for proofreading parts of my original disseration. I am also grateful to the secretaries, the non-scientific employees of the institute, and the helpdesk team.

I also acknowledge the Max-Planck Center for Visual Computing and Communication, the International Max-Planck Research School for Computer Science, and the EU-Project 3DTV within FP6 under Grant 511568 for their partial financial support during my PhD studies.

Finally, I would like to thank my whole family and in particular my parents, Aparicio de Aguiar and Maria Auxiliadora de Aguiar, who always encouraged and supported me.

Contents

Part IV: Processing Mesh Animations

Chapter 1
Introduction

This book presents methods for the realistic generation of virtual doubles of real-world actors. First, two efficient mesh-based alternatives to simplify the overall character animation process are proposed. Thereafter, three passive performance capture methods are presented dealing with actors wearing arbitrary everyday apparel. At the end, two novel algorithms for processing mesh animations are described. As a whole, the methods presented here form a powerful system to accurately capture, manipulate and realistically render real-world human performances, exceeding the capabilities of many related capture techniques.

While the technology to render and model scene environments with landscapes and buildings, natural phenomena like water and fire, and plants has reached a high level of maturity in computer graphics, it is still hard to authentically create virtual doubles of real-world actors. One recent example illustrating this fact is the photo-realistic CGI movie Beowulf [12]. Only by capitalizing on recent advances in shape acquisition, marker-based motion capture, and by drawing from the talent of a large team of animators, it became possible to finish the movie within an allowable time frame. Nonetheless, the high production costs illustrate that the price to be paid are millions of man hours of tedious manual editing and post-processing.

In order to obtain a realistic virtual actor, it is important that he/she mimics as closely as possible the motion of his/her real-world counterpart. It is thus no wonder that the number of working hours that animators spend in order to live up to these high requirements in visual quality is considerable. For generating virtual people, animators commonly use the traditional skeleton-based animation pipeline: first, a kinematic skeleton model is implanted into the geometry of the human model [10]. Thereafter, the skeleton is attached to the surface [11]. Finally, a description of the motion in terms of joint parameters of the skeleton is required. It can either be manually designed or learned from a real person by means of motion capture [9, 14].

Although the interplay of all these steps delivers realistic animations, the whole process is still very expensive and tedious. In this book, we first describe two

E. de Aguiar: Animation & Performance Capture Using Digi. Models, COSMOS 5, pp. 1–5.
springerlink.com

versatile, fast and simple alternatives to attack this problem that aim at simplifying the overall animation process. Our methods streamline the whole pipeline from laser-scanning to animation from motion capture, and can be directly integrated into the traditional animation workflow.

Another complex problem in computer graphics is to capture the time-varying dynamic geometry of actors in the real world. Currently, marker-based and marker-free motion capture systems only measure the subject's motion in terms of a kinematic skeleton. If a dynamic representation is required, motion capture approaches need to be combined with other special techniques [8, 15, 13]. However, as these methods demand the actors to wear skin-tight body suits, it remains impossible to record performances under natural conditions, such as in normal clothing.

To bridge this gap, we also present in this book three algorithmic alternatives to capture the motion and the time-varying shape deformations of people wearing even wide everyday apparel and performing fast and complex motions. This is achieved by combining an efficient mesh-deformation method and a tracking framework based on image cues in multi-view video sequences. The proposed methods achieve a high level of flexibility and versatility by explicitly abandoning any traditional skeletal parametrization and by posing *performance capture* as deformation capture. Moreover, they enable us to record the subject's appearance, which can be used to display the recorded actor from arbitrary viewpoints, and to produce a spatio-temporally coherence dynamic representation that can be easily made available to animators.

By using our novel performance capture techniques, we offer a great level of flexibility during animation creation. However, currently there is only a limited number of techniques that are able to post-process and modify the generated mesh animations. To overcome this limitation, in this book we also propose two novel algorithms for processing mesh animations. The first approach enables the fully-automatic conversion of a mesh animation into a skeleton-based animation that can be easily edited by animators. The second one automatically converts a mesh animation into an animation collage, i.e. a moving assembly of 3D shape primitives from a database. Together, they are important contributions to the animator toolbox with a variety of applications in visual arts, movie and game productions.

Each method described here can be regarded as a solution to a particular problem or as a building block that enables the development of novel interesting applications. All together, they also create a powerful system to accurately capture, manipulate and realistically render real-world human performances, going beyond the limits of related capture techniques. The methods described in this book are usually tailored to deal with human actors. However, the fundamental principles can also be applied to a larger class of scenes, as described in the respective chapters.

1.1   Main Contributions and Organization of the Book

This book contains 16 chapters and it is divided into four parts, each of which focuses on one major algorithmic subproblem. In the first part (Chapters 2, 3 and

4) some technical and theoretical background information needed to understand the following projects is provided. After that, we begin describing the main contributions of this work in the second part (Chapters 5, 6 and 7), where two efficient and easy-to-use solutions to directly animate a laser-scanned model from marker-based or marker-less motion capture data are presented. These methods can be considered alternatives to the complex traditional skeleton-based character animation pipeline.

Thereafter, the third part of the book (Chapters 8, 9, 10, 11 and 12) describes three alternative solutions to directly and realistically create a virtual double of a moving real-world actor, by capturing its time-varying geometry using a mesh-deformation method from unaltered video footage. By using this high-quality captured performance, we are also able to display the recorded actor from arbitrary viewpoints. In the last part of the book (Chapters 13, 14 and 15), we propose two novel approaches for processing mesh animations acquired by our performance captured methods or generated by animators.

We conclude in Chapter 16 with a description of possible future work. The methods and algorithms described in this book have been published before in a variety of peer-reviewed conference and journal articles. The main scientific contributions as well as the appropriate references are briefly summarized in the following sections.

1.1.1 Part I - Background and Basic Definitions

We begin in Chapter 2 by describing how a real-world camera, and the kinematics, the shape and the appearance of a real-world subject can be modeled in a computer. Afterwards, important computer vision algorithms that are employed by several projects in the book are described.

Chapter 3 details the interactive shape deformation and editing techniques that are also employed by several projects in the book. These methods are able to efficiently manipulate the input scanned model as naturally as possible, generating physically plausible and aesthetically pleasing deformation results.

Finally, Chapter 4 presents our recording setup that provides high quality data for the different projects proposed in the book. The details of the main components of our studio and all necessary recording steps to generate the multi-view video data are described.

1.1.2 Part II - Natural Animation of Digitized Models

Animators are able to generate photo-realistic animations using their well-established but often inflexible set of tools. However, the skeleton-based paradigm still requires a high amount of manual interaction. In Chapter 5, we first describe the drawbacks of the traditional skeleton-based character animation pipeline. Thereafter, we review the most important related work on character animation, as well as possible solutions to simplify the overall animation process.

Chapter 6 and 7 present two versatile, fast and simple methods that streamline the whole pipeline from laser-scanning to character animation [4, 6, 7]. Although the algorithms abandon the concept of a kinematic skeleton, they integrate into the traditional animation workflow and enable animators to quickly produce convincing animation results with minimal manual effort.

1.1.3 Part III - Towards Performance Capture Using Deformable Mesh Tracking

Stepping directly from a captured real-world sequence to the corresponding realistic moving character is still a challenging task. In chapter 8, we first introduce our three solutions to attack this problem. Thereafter, we review the closely related work in human motion capture, dynamic scene reconstruction, and 3D video.

Chapter 9 presents the first alternative to accurately and automatically track the motion and time-varying non-rigid surface deformations of people wearing every-day apparel from a handful of multi-view video streams. This is achieved by combining an optical flow-based 3D correspondence estimation technique with a fast Laplacian-based tracking scheme [3].

Chapter 10 presents a second alternative that combines a flow-based and an image-feature based tracking method. Furthermore, we divide the problem into two steps: first, a simple and robust method is proposed to automatically identify and track features on arbitrary subjects. Thereafter, using the 3D trajectories of the features, an efficient Laplacian-based tracking scheme is used to realistically animate a static human body scan over time [2].

Chapter 11 presents our more advanced video-based performance capture system that passively reconstructs spatio-temporally coherent shape, motion, and texture of actors at an unprecedented quality [1]. The approach combines a new skeleton-less shape deformation method, a new marker-less analysis-through-synthesis framework for pose recovery, and a new model-guided multi-view stereo approach for shape refinement, thereby exceeding the capabilities of many related capturing approaches.

Finally, in Chapter 12, we present a system to render high-quality 3D Videos that enables convincing display of human subjects from arbitrary synthetic viewpoints. Our approach combines our detailed dynamic scene representation with a projective texture method [1] and leads to a better visual quality as compared to previous approaches.

1.1.4 Part IV - Processing Mesh Animations

Animators are used to a large repertoire of tools for editing and rendering traditional skeletal animations, but yet lack the same set of tools for working with mesh animations, i.e. our mesh-based dynamic scene representations. In Chapter 13, we first introduce two novel approaches for processing mesh animations. Afterwards, we review the closely related work in mesh segmentation, skeleton reconstruction, character skinning, mesh animation editing, and shape matching.

Chapter 14 presents our first algorithm to process mesh animations. We describe an algorithm to fully-automatically extract a skeleton structure, skeletal motion parameters, and surface skinning weights from arbitrary deforming mesh sequences, thereby enabling easy post-processing and fast rendering of mesh animations with standard skeleton-based tools [5].

The second method for post-processing mesh animations is presented in Chapter 15. Our system is able to automatically transform mesh animations into animation collages, i.e. a complete reassembly of the original animation in a new abstract visual style that imitates the spatio-temporal shape and deformation of the input [16].

References

1. de Aguiar, E., Stoll, C., Theobalt, C., Ahmed, N., Seidel, H.P., Thrun, S.: Performance capture from sparse multi-view video. In: ACM TOG, Proc. SIGGRAPH (2008)
2. de Aguiar, E., Theobalt, C., Stoll, C., Seidel, H.: Marker-less 3d feature tracking for mesh-based human motion capture. In: Proc. ICCV HUMO 2007, pp. 1–15 (2007)
3. de Aguiar, E., Theobalt, C., Stoll, C., Seidel, H.P.: Marker-less deformable mesh tracking for human shape and motion capture. In: Proc. CVPR (2007)
4. de Aguiar, E., Theobalt, C., Stoll, C., Seidel, H.P.: Rapid animation of laser-scanned humans. In: IEEE Virtual Reality 2007, pp. 223–226 (2007)
5. de Aguiar, E., Theobalt, C., Thrun, S., Seidel, H.P.: Automatic conversion of mesh animations into skeleton-based animations. Computer Graphics Forum (Proc. Eurographics EG 2008) 27(2), 389–397 (2008)
6. de Aguiar, E., Zayer, R., Theobalt, C., Magnor, M., Seidel, H.P.: A simple framework for natural animation of digitized models. In: IEEE SIBGRAPI (2007)
7. de Aguiar, E., Zayer, R., Theobalt, C., Magnor, M., Seidel, H.P.: Video-driven animation of human body scans. In: IEEE 3DTV Conference (2007)
8. Allen, B., Curless, B., Popović, Z.: Articulated body deformation from range scan data. ACM Trans. Graph. 21(3), 612–619 (2002)
9. Bodenheimer, B., Rose, C., Rosenthal, S., Pella, J.: The process of motion capture: Dealing with the data. In: Computer Animation and Simulation 1997, pp. 3–18 (1997)
10. Herda, L., Fua, P., Plänkers, R., Boulic, R., Thalmann, D.: Skeleton-based motion capture for robust reconstruction of human motion. In: CA 2000: Proc. of the Computer Animation, p. 77 (2000)
11. Lewis, J.P., Cordner, M., Fong, N.: Pose space deformation: a unified approach to shape interpolation and skeleton-driven deformation. In: Proc. of ACM SIGGRAPH 2000, pp. 165–172 (2000)
12. Paramount: Beowulf (2007), http://www.beowulfmovie.com/
13. Park, S.I., Hodgins, J.K.: Capturing and animating skin deformation in human motion. ACM Transactions on Graphics (SIGGRAPH 2006) 25(3), 881–889 (2006)
14. Poppe, R.: Vision-based human motion analysis: An overview. CVIU 108, 4–18 (2007)
15. Sand, P., McMillan, L., Popović, J.: Continuous capture of skin deformation. ACM Trans. Graph. 22(3), 578–586 (2003)
16. Theobalt, C., Rössl, C., de Aguiar, E., Seidel, H.P.: Animation collage. In: SCA 2007, pp. 271–280 (2007)

Part I
Background and Basic Definitions

Chapter 2
Preliminary Techniques

In this chapter, first some general theoretical background information about camera and human models are given. Thereafter, elementary computer vision techniques that many of the projects in this book capitalize on are described.

Several projects described in this book have synchronized multiple video streams as input, Chapter 4. Therefore, in order to correctly simulate the imaging process of the cameras in a computer, a mathematical camera model is required. Such formulation is detailed in Sect. 2.1, where the correspondence between a real camera and its computational equivalent is presented. After that, we briefly describe the process of camera calibration and the imaging geometry of stereo cameras.

The description of how we model the shape, kinematics and appearance of a real-world subject in a computer is detailed in Sect. 2.2. Although the projects in this book are usually tailored to human actors, the fundamental principles described here can also be applied to a larger class of real-world subjects, like animals.

This chapter concludes in Sect. 2.3 with a description of important computer vision algorithms employed by several projects proposed in this book. In particular, we briefly describe how to perform background subtraction, and how to calculate optical flow, scene flow and SIFT features.

2.1 The Camera Model

The information contained in a 3D scene can be captured to a 2D image plane by a camera as follows: first, a lens collects the incident illumination. Afterwards, the light rays are deflected towards a focal point, and at the end, the deflected rays create an image of the observed scene. In the following sections, we will describe the mathematical framework for mapping the 3D world space to the 2D image plane, the process of camera calibration and the geometry of stereo cameras.

2.1.1 Mathematical Model

A pinhole camera model describes the image formation process of a camera by a projective linear transformation [5]. Let $\overline{p}_{wo} = (p_x, p_y, p_z, 1)^T$ be a point specified

E. de Aguiar: Animation & Performance Capture Using Digi. Models, COSMOS 5, pp. 9–18.
springerlink.com   © Springer-Verlag Berlin Heidelberg 2010

in the world coordinate frame, Fig. 2.1. Its projected location in the image plane $\bar{p}_{im}$ of the camera evaluates to:

$$\bar{p}_{im} = KO\bar{p}_{wo} = \begin{bmatrix} \alpha_x & 0 & x_0 \\ 0 & \alpha_y & y_0 \\ 0 & 0 & 1 \end{bmatrix} \begin{bmatrix} R & -Rc \\ 0 & 1 \end{bmatrix} \bar{p}_{wo} \tag{2.1}$$

In Eq. 2.1, R is a 3×3 rotation matrix that represents the orientation of the camera's local coordinate frame with respect to the world coordinate frame and $c \in \mathbb{R}^3$ is the Euclidean world coordinate of the camera's center of projection. The parameters R and c are called the external or extrinsic parameters of the camera. The matrix K can be referred to as the calibration matrix and its entries are called the intrinsic parameters of the camera. The principal point in the image plane is at position (x_0, y_0), at the intersection of the optical axis with the image plane. The coefficients $\alpha_x = fm_x$ and $\alpha_y = fm_y$ represent the focal length of the camera in terms of pixel dimensions in x and y directions, respectively. The focal length f of the camera, and m_x and m_y represent the number of pixels per unit distance in image coordinates in x and y respectively. Therefore, a real-world camera can be represented by 10 parameters.

However, unfortunately the physical properties of lenses make the previous image formation process geometrically deviate from the ideal pinhole model. Geometric deviations are typically caused by radial or tangential distortion artifacts [8]. Radial distortion happens since a real lens bents light rays towards the optical center by more or less than the ideal amount. Tangential distortion are caused by the bad alignment of the individual lenses in an optical system with respect to the overall optical axis [16].

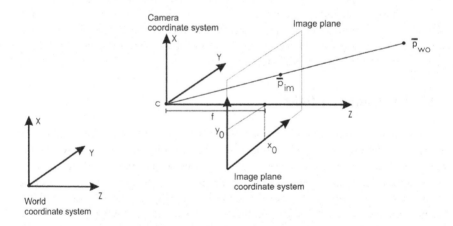

Fig. 2.1 The imaging process of a real-world camera is simulated by the mathematical camera model.

2.1.2 Camera Calibration

Camera calibration is the process of determining the parameters of the mathematical model that optimally reflect the geometric and photometric imaging properties of the real camera. The most important calibration step is the geometric calibration, where the parameters of the imaging model detailed in Sect. 2.1.1 are estimated. The majority of the calibration algorithms [14, 8, 6] take into account radial and tangential lens distortions and derive these parameters from images of a calibration object with known physical dimensions, such as a checkerboard pattern, Sect. 4.3.1.1. The parameters are estimated by means of an optimization procedure that modifies the model parameters until the predicted appearance of the calibration object optimally aligns with the captured images.

Additionally, color calibration can be applied to ensure correct color reproduction under a given illumination setup. White balancing is the simplest color calibration procedure that computes multiplicative scaling factors from an image of a purely white or gray object. In our projects, we also developed a more sophisticated relative calibration procedure that assure color-consistency across the cameras, Sect. 4.3.1.2.

2.1.3 Geometry of Stereo Cameras

A stereo camera comprises of a pair of cameras whose viewing directions converge, and it can be used to derive 3D structural information about the scene. If both cameras are fully-calibrated (intrinsic and extrinsic parameters), the 3D position of a point p visible in both cameras can be calculated via triangulation, Fig. 2.2(a). The position p is estimated by computing the intersection point of two rays, r_A and r_B. The ray r_A originates in the center of projection of camera A, c_A, and passes the image plane in the position p_A. The same construction is valid for ray r_B from camera B. However, due to measurement noise, the rays will not intersect exactly at a single point. In this case, we can compute a pseudo-intersection point that minimizes the sum of squared distance to each pointing ray.

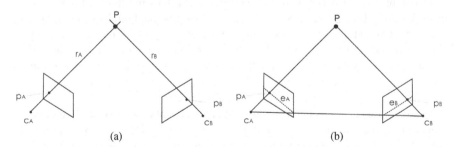

(a) (b)

Fig. 2.2 Geometry of stereo cameras: **(a)** Triangulation - the 3D position of a point p is calculated by the intersection of the two rays, r_A and r_B, through the respective cameras' centers of projection, c_A and c_B, and the respective projected image plane positions, p_A and p_B. **(b)** Epipolar geometry - The point p_A in camera A corresponds to the point p_B in camera B that lies in the epipolar line e_B.

The epipolar geometry describes the image formation process in a stereo pair of cameras, Fig. 2.2(b). It describes the fact that an image point p_A in camera view A has a corresponding point p_B in the camera view B, which lies on a line e_B in image B, the so-called epipolar line. The epipolar geometry of a stereo pair is fully-specified by its fundamental matrix. The fundamental matrix can be inferred from 8 point correspondences between two uncalibrated cameras, and it is directly available for fully-calibrated camera pairs [4, 5]. By using the fundamental matrix and the epipolar line, image correspondences can be computed using simple matrix multiplications, which reduces the problem to an one-dimensional search space along a line.

2.2 Modeling Humans

The appearance, and the physical and kinematic properties of a real-world human body are the result of the interplay of many complex physiological components. For example, the appearance of the skin is the result of structural pigmentation, light interaction on the body surface, and the deformation of muscles and connective tissues. The kinematic properties of the human body are mainly determined by its skeleton structure, i.e. bones and interconnecting joints. The kinematics also influences the physical shape of the person. Therefore, an authentic computational human model has to realistically represent the shape, kinematics and appearance of the real human. Such representations are described in the following sections.

2.2.1 Modeling the Shape

The surface geometry of the human body is typically modeled by means of a triangle mesh. A mesh is a collection of vertices, edges and faces that defines the shape of an object in computer graphics. The faces usually consist of triangles, which are connected by their common edges.

In our projects, we acquired the geometric details of the human body by using a full body laser scanner, Sect. 4.2.4. Our computational model of the shape is obtained by transforming the raw scans, i.e. triangulated depth maps, into a high-quality surface mesh employing a Poisson reconstruction method [9]. By using such scanning device, we are able to capture not only the coarse shape of the actor, but also fine details in the body shape and in the apparel. Moreover, such acquisition technology enables us to easily model different subjects.

In most projects in this book, we abandon the concept of a kinematic skeleton to represent the motion and deformations of the virtual actor. By doing this, our novel algorithms rely mostly on the high-quality model of the actor's shape to simultaneously capture rigid and non-rigidly deforming surfaces from multiple synchronized video streams.

2.2.2 Modeling the Appearance

Another important component contributing to a realistic look of a virtual human is the surface texture. A possible way to reproduce the appearance of a real-world actor is to reconstruct a consistent surface texture from images showing the subject. However, a static texture cannot reproduce dynamic details, such as wrinkles in the apparel.

In our projects, we use dynamic surface textures that incorporate such time-varying details. The multiple video streams are recorded in our studio by cameras providing high frame-rates, high resolution and precise color reproduction, Chapter 4. Therefore, realistic virtual actors are generated by combining the multiple synchronized footage with the model's pose at each particular frame, Chapter 12.

2.2.3 Modeling the Kinematics

The computational equivalent of the human skeleton is a kinematic skeleton, that mathematically models a hierarchical arrangement of joints and interconnecting bones [13]. The human skeleton is usually approximated by a collection of kinematic sub-chains, where the relative orientation between one segment and the subsequent one in the hierarchy is controlled via a rigid body transformation. It jointly describes a rotational and a translational transformation between the local coordinate frames of adjacent rigid bodies.

The translational components of the rigid body transformations are implicitly represented by the bone lengths and the joints model the rotational components. Since the bone lengths are constant, the pose of the skeleton is fully-specified by the rotation parameters for each joint and an additional translational parameter for the root. Such kinematic models are automatically learned from arbitrary mesh animations in Chapter 14.

2.3 Computer Vision Algorithms

2.3.1 Background Subtraction

In the projects described in this book, a method to robustly segment a person in the foreground of a scene from the background is necessary. Due to its robustness, we decided to use the color-based method originally proposed in [3], which incorporates an additional criterion to prevent shadows from being erroneously classified as part of the scene foreground. The technique employs per-pixel color statistics for each background pixel that is represented by a mean image $\Pi = \{\mu(x,y) \mid 0 \leq x < \text{width}, 0 \leq y < \text{height}\}$ and a standard-deviation image $\Sigma = \{\sigma(x,y) \mid 0 \leq x < \text{width}, 0 \leq y < \text{height}\}$, with each pixel value being a 3-vector comprising all three color channels. The statistics is generated from consecutive input image frames of the background scene without an object in the foreground, in order to incorporate the pixel intensity variations due to noise and natural illumination changes.

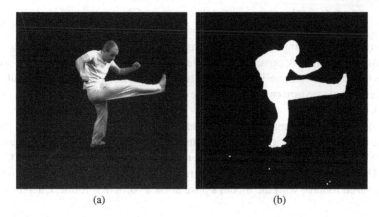

(a)   (b)

Fig. 2.3 Background subtraction: input image frame (**a**) and the corresponding silhouette mask (**b**). Our background subtraction method correctly segments the foreground subject from the background.

The background subtraction method classifies an image pixel $p(p_x, p_y)$ as foreground if the color of $p(p_x, p_y)$ differs in at least one RGB channel by more than an upper threshold T_u from the background distribution

$$| p(p_x, p_y)_c - \mu(p_x, p_y)_c | > T_u \cdot \sigma(p_x, p_y)_c, \ c \in \{r, g, b\} \tag{2.2}$$

If this difference is smaller than the lower threshold T_l in all channels, it is classified as a background pixel. All pixels which fall in between these thresholds are possibly in shadow areas and can be classified depending on the amount of variation in the hue value. The difference in hue can be calculated as

$$\Delta = \cos^{-1} \left(\frac{p(p_x, p_y) \cdot \mu(p_x, p_y)}{\|p(p_x, p_y)\| \|\mu(p_x, p_y)\|} \right). \tag{2.3}$$

If $\Delta > T_{ang}$, the pixel is classified as foreground, otherwise as background. At the end, a 0/1-silhouette mask image for each input video frame is computed, Fig. 2.3.

2.3.2 Optical Flow

Optical flow is the projection of the 3D motion field of a real-world dynamic scene into the 2D image plane of a recording camera. Algorithms used to calculate optical flow attempt to find correlations between adjacent frames, generating a vector field showing where each pixel or region in one frame moved to in the next frame.

In computer vision, a number of simplifying assumptions are usually made to compute the optical flow from the pixel intensities of two consecutive images. The basic assumption is that the pixel intensity does not significantly change between two subsequent frames, the so-called intensity constancy constraint:

$$I(u,t) = I(u - \mathbf{o}t, 0), \tag{2.4}$$

where $\mathbf{o} = (p,q)^T$ is the optical flow at image point $u = (u,v)^T$, and $I(u,t)$ is the image intensity at coordinates (u,v) and time t. As a pixel at location $(u,v)^T$ with intensity $I(u,t)$ moves by δ_u between two frames, the intensity constraint equation can be formulated as follows:

$$I(u,t) = I(u + \delta_u, t + \delta_t). \tag{2.5}$$

From the Taylor series approximations, Eq. 2.5 leads to:

$$\nabla I(u,t) \cdot \mathbf{o} + I_t(u,t) = 0, \tag{2.6}$$

where $I_t(u,t)$ is the temporal derivative of the image intensity. In order to make the problem well-posed, additional assumptions need to be made about the smoothness of the optical flow field in a local spatial neighborhood.

In the differential optical flow approach by Lucas and Kanade [12], the flow is assumed to be constant in a small neighborhood. The solution is achieved by minimizing the following functional

$$\sum_{u \in W} W^2(u) [\nabla I(u,t) \cdot \mathbf{o} + I_t(u,t)]^2, \tag{2.7}$$

where $W(u)$ defines a Gaussian neighborhood around the current position in the image plane for which the optical flow is computed. Alternatively, a hierarchical variant can be employed that incorporates flow estimates from multiple levels of an image pyramid into its final result.

Using the same basic formulation, a large number of algorithms have been proposed in the literature. In general, they are based on the Horn-Schunck model [7], that additionally uses a global smoothness constraint to regularize the optical flow computation. An example is the dense optical flow method by Black et al. [1]. The approach is based on a statistical framework that enables the robust estimation of flow fields addressing violations of the intensity constancy and spatial smoothness assumptions. As a result, the method is able to deal with discontinuities in the flow field.

Recently, Brox et al. [2] proposed a multiresolution warping-based method for dense optical flow that uses a continuous, rotationally invariant energy functional. The energy functional $E(u,v)$ is composed by a weighted sum between a data term $E_D(u,v)$ and a smoothing term $E_S(u,v)$ as follows:

$$E(u,v) = E_D(u,v) + \alpha E_S(u,v).$$

The data term contains the intensity constancy assumption, as in Eq. 2.4, and a gradient constancy assumption described by $\nabla I(u,t) = \nabla I(u - \mathbf{o}t, 0)$, which makes the framework susceptible to slight changes in brightness. By this means, the overall energy functional becomes more robust against intensity value changes. The smoothness term $E_S(u,v)$ takes into account neighboring information to improve the calculation of the flow field by penalizing its total variation.

The global minimum solution is found via a multiscale approach. One starts by solving a coarse, smoothed version of the problem. Thereafter, the coarse solution is used as initialization for solving a refined version of the problem until step by step the original problem is solved. Additionally, the energy functional $E(u,v)$ is designed using the non-linearized data terms and linearizations are computed during the numerical scheme used to solve it. By this means, the overall method improves the convergence of the solution to the global minimum, generating more accurate results.

2.3.3 Scene Flow

The scene flow is a three-dimensional flow field describing the motion of every 3D point in the scene. Following [15], we consider $x = x(t)$ the 3D path of a point in the world, and $\frac{dx}{dt}$ its instantaneous scene flow. If the image of this point in camera C_i is $u_i = u_i(t)$, the optical flow $\mathbf{o} = \frac{du_i}{dt}$ is the projection of the scene flow into the image plane:

$$\frac{du_i}{dt} = \frac{\partial u_i}{\partial x}\frac{dx}{dt}, \tag{2.8}$$

where $\frac{\partial u_i}{\partial x}$ is the 2×3 Jacobian matrix that represents the differential relationship between x and u_i.

The Eq. 2.8 expresses the fact that any optical flow $\frac{du_i}{dt}$ is the projection of the scene flow $\frac{dx}{dt}$. Therefore, assuming that the optical flow has been computed for a particular point in the scene for two or more camera views, the scene flow can be recovered.

If $N > 2$ cameras see a particular point, the solution that minimizes the sum of least squares of the error can be obtained by reprojecting the scene flow onto each of the optical flows. Therefore, the values of $\frac{dx_j}{dt}$ can be calculated by solving the system of equations $B\frac{dx_j}{dt} = U$ via singular value decomposition, where

$$B = \begin{bmatrix} \frac{\partial u_1}{\partial x} & \frac{\partial u_1}{\partial y} & \frac{\partial u_1}{\partial z} \\ \frac{\partial v_1}{\partial x} & \frac{\partial v_1}{\partial y} & \frac{\partial v_1}{\partial z} \\ \cdot & \cdot & \cdot \\ \cdot & \cdot & \cdot \\ \frac{\partial u_N}{\partial x} & \frac{\partial u_N}{\partial y} & \frac{\partial u_N}{\partial z} \\ \frac{\partial v_N}{\partial x} & \frac{\partial v_N}{\partial y} & \frac{\partial v_N}{\partial z} \end{bmatrix}, \ U = \begin{bmatrix} \frac{\partial u_1}{\partial t} \\ \frac{\partial v_1}{\partial t} \\ \cdot \\ \cdot \\ \frac{\partial u_N}{\partial t} \\ \frac{\partial v_N}{\partial t} \end{bmatrix}.$$

2.3.4 Image Features

A feature is an interesting part of an image that is commonly used to guide many computer vision algorithms. Once a feature is detected, a local image patch around it can be extracted and a feature descriptor or feature vector can be computed. An important algorithm to detect and describe local features in images is the Scale-invariant feature transform (or SIFT) [10, 11]. The SIFT features are local, and invariant to image scale and rotation. They are also robust to changes in illumination, noise, occlusion, and viewpoint.

The method begins by detecting interest points, also called keypoints. For this, the image is convolved with Gaussian filters at different scales, and the difference of successive Gaussian-blurred images are considered. Keypoints are chosen as maxima/minima of the Difference of Gaussians (DoG) that occur at multiple scales. Specifically, a DoG image $D(\sigma)$ is given by

$$D(\sigma) = L(k_i\sigma) - L(k_j\sigma), \tag{2.9}$$

where $L(k\sigma) = G(k\sigma) * I$ is the original image I convolved with the Gaussian blur $G(k\sigma)$ at scale $k\sigma$.

Unfortunately, the previous step produces too many keypoint candidates, some of which are unstable. Therefore, the algorithm discards low contrast keypoints and filters out those located on edges. Afterwards, each remaining keypoint is assigned one or more orientations based on local image gradient directions. This enables invariance to rotation as a keypoint descriptor can be represented relative to this orientation.

At the end, descriptor vectors are computed for these keypoints such that they are highly distinctive and partially invariant to illumination and viewpoint. The feature descriptor is computed as a set of orientation histograms on a 4×4 pixel neighborhood, yielding a feature vector with 128 elements.

References

1. Black, M., Anandan, P.: A framework for the robust estimation of optical flow. In: Proc. of ICCV, pp. 231–236 (1993)
2. Brox, T., Bruhn, A., Papenberg, N., Weickert, J.: High accuracy optical flow estimation based on a theory for warping. In: Pajdla, T., Matas, J(G.) (eds.) ECCV 2004. LNCS, vol. 3024, pp. 25–36. Springer, Heidelberg (2004)
3. Cheung, G., Kanade, T., Bouguet, J.Y., Holler, M.: A real time system for robust 3D voxel reconstruction of human motions. In: Proc. of CVPR, vol. 2, pp. 714–720 (2000)
4. Faugeras, O.: Three-Dimensional Computer Vision: a Geometric Viewpoint. MIT Press, Cambridge (1993)
5. Hartley, R., Zisserman, A.: Multiple View Geometry in Computer Vision. Cambridge University Press, Cambridge (2000)
6. Heikkila, J., Silven, O.: Calibration procedure for short focal length off-the-shelf ccd cameras. In: Proc. of 13th ICPR, pp. 166–170 (1996)
7. Horn, B.K.P., Schunck, B.G.: Determining optical flow. Artificial Intelligence 17, 185–203 (1981)

8. Jain, R., Kasturi, R., Schunck, B.G.: Machine Vision. McGraw Hill International, New York (1995)
9. Kazhdan, M., Bolitho, M., Hoppe, H.: Poisson surface reconstruction. In: Proc. SGP, pp. 61–70 (2006)
10. Lowe, D.G.: Object recognition from local scale-invariant features. In: Proc. of ICCV, pp. 1150–1157 (1999)
11. Lowe, D.G.: Distinctive image features from scale-invariant keypoints. In: IJCV, vol. 20, pp. 91–110 (2004)
12. Lucas, B., Kanade, T.: An iterative image registration technique with an application to stereo vision. In: Proc. DARPA IU Workshop, pp. 121–130 (1981)
13. Murray, R.M., Li, Z., Sastry, S.S.: A Mathematical Introduction to Robotic Manipulation. CRC Press, Boca Raton (1994)
14. Tsai, R.Y.: An efficient and accurate camera calibration technique for 3d machine vision. In: Proc. of CVPR, pp. 364–374 (1986)
15. Vedula, S., Baker, S., Rander, P., Collins, R., Kanade, T.: Three-dimensional scene flow. IEEE PAMI 27(3), 475–480 (2005)
16. Weng, J., Cohen, P., Herniou, M.: Calibration of stereo cameras using a non-linear distortion model. In: ICPR, pp. 246–253 (1990)

Chapter 3
Interactive Shape Deformation and Editing Methods

This chapter reviews the most relevant work on interactive shape deformation and editing techniques, and describes the three main deformation approaches used in this book.

In recent years, interactive shape deformation and editing techniques have become an active field of research in computer graphics, Sect. 3.1. Commonly, the input to such techniques is a triangle mesh to be deformed, denoted by $\mathcal{M}_{tri} = (V_{tri}, T_{tri})$, which consists of n vertices $V_{tri} = \{v_1 \cdots v_n\}$ and m triangles $T_{tri} = \{t_1 \cdots t_m\}$. The goal is the development of algorithms to efficiently edit and manipulate $\mathcal{M}_{tri}$ as naturally as possible under the influence of a set of constraints specified by the user.

Physical simulation [22] and non-linear deformation methods [25, 7] are able to deliver accurate and physically-correct deformation results. However, unfortunately these methods require the minimization of complex non-linear energies, which often makes them difficult to implement and computationally too expensive to be used in an interactive environment, where different constraints are used to update and correct the shape of a model on-the-fly.

In general, in order to be interactive, editing methods need to be based on easy-to-compute linear deformations that still generate physically plausible and aesthetically pleasing deformation results, i.e. deformations should be smooth or piecewise smooth and the result should preserve the local appearance of the surface under deformation. Recently, linear deformation methods based on differential representations have gained more popularity because they are fast to compute, robust, and easy to implement, as the associated linear system is sparse. Instead of directly modify the spatial location of each vertex in the model, they use a local differential representation of the shape, which encodes information about its local shape and the size and orientation of the local details, to obtain a detail-preserving deformation result. Deformation is performed by constructing a differential representation of the shape, manipulating it according to the given constraints, and finally reconstructing the shape from the modified differential representation. While sharing the same general framework, the two main categories of differential techniques differ by the

E. de Aguiar: Animation & Performance Capture Using Digi. Models, COSMOS 5, pp. 19–27.
springerlink.com   © Springer-Verlag Berlin Heidelberg 2010

particular representation they use: deformation gradients, Sect. 3.2.1, or Laplacian coordinates, Sect. 3.2.2.

In general, when applying these methods, the resulting deformation is dependent on the particular embedding of the surface in space. During model manipulation, its local representation is not updated, which may lead to unnatural deformations. This happens since the surface deformation problem is inherently non-linear, as it requires the estimation of local rotations to be applied to the local differential representations. To correct this limitation in the linearization process, many approaches were developed in the last years attacking this problem from different directions, Sect. 3.1. After reviewing the most relevant related work on interactive shape deformation techniques in the next section, we first present two surface-based techniques used later in this book: the guided Poisson-based approach and the guided Laplacian-based technique, Sect. 3.2.1 and Sect. 3.2.2 respectively. Thereafter, an iterative volumetric approach is described, Sect 3.3. As can be seen later, the mesh deformation techniques presented in this chapter are key components for the advanced methods proposed in this book.

3.1 Related Work

Interactive shape editing is an important field of research in computer graphics, and consequently a variety of different solutions were proposed to solve this problem [9]. Early methods like free-form deformation [24] or space deformations [5, 21] enable high-quality shape modeling by directly manipulating the 3D space where the object is embedded. However, they typically fail to reproduce correct deformation results if only a small number of constraints is used.

Some approaches propose to solve the computationally expensive non-linear surface deformation problem directly. [25, 17] propose a non-linear differential coordinate setup, while [7] minimizes bending and stretching energies using a coupled shell of prisms. [15] employs a non-linear version of the volumetric graph Laplacian and [33] presents an extension of the non-linear Poisson-based deformation approach applied to mesh sequences. Alternatively, [4] proposes a non-linear handle-aware isoline technique and [26] combines Laplacian-based deformation with skeleton-based inverse kinematics. In general, the main limitation of these non-linear methods is often that interactive deformation is only feasible on models of reduced complexity.

Interactive performance for more complex objects can be achieved by simplifying the inherent non-linear problem. One way to preserve geometric details under global deformations is to use multi-resolution techniques [38, 16, 14, 18, 6]. While these approaches are an effective tool for enhancing fine-scale detail preservation, the generation of the hierarchy can be expensive for complex models. Moreover, it is hard to deal with large deformations in a single step. These limitations are the main reason for differential-based deformation approaches, which represent the model using its local differential coordinates instead of using its spatial coordinates.

Typically, two differential representations can be used: deformation gradients or Laplacian coordinates. Poisson-based methods use the input transformation constraints given by the user to modify the surface gradients of the model. [35] presents a Poisson-based mesh editing method where the local transformations are propagated based on the geodesic distances. [36] replaces the geodesic propagation scheme by harmonic field interpolation and shows that this leads to a better estimation of the local transformations. [23] extends the harmonic field interpolation scheme to deal with different materials. Unfortunately, although these methods work well for rotations, since they are handled explicitly, they are insensitive to translations.

Laplacian-based methods represent vertex coordinates relative to their neighbors in the model [3]. Although the original framework can not correctly deal with rotations, recent improvements allow the methods to work similarly well for translations and rotations. [19] describes how local rotations can be estimated and incorporated to the original framework. [30] proposes to use the Laplacian representation combined with implicit transformation optimization. [11] presents a hybrid scheme combining implicit optimization with a two-step local transformation estimation. In general, although these methods are able to estimate local rotations, the required linearization yields artifacts for large rotations.

Generally, most of these methods suffer from linearization problems: methods which use translational constraints are insensitive to rotations, whereas methods relying on rotational constraints exhibit insensitivity to translations. To solve this problem, recent methods use skeleton-based techniques [34], multi-step approaches [10], or iterative approaches [29].

Most linear deformation methods rely on a triangle mesh representation. However, deforming a surface model may cause local self intersections and shrinking effects. To prevent such artifacts, some methods use a volumetric structure as basis for the linear deformation [37, 31].

Another class of approaches is able to manipulate an object while guaranteeing volume preservation by defining deformations based on vector fields [12]. Although it enables the definition of advanced implicit deformation tools, it is still hard to construct vector fields that satisfy the user-defined constraints.

3.2 Mesh Editing Techniques

In this section, we review the two surface-based deformation techniques based on differential representations and describe the respective steps needed to reconstruct the deformed surfaces.

3.2.1 Guided Poisson-Based Method

Inputs to this method are a static triangle mesh $\mathcal{M}_{tri}$ and affine transformations (rotation and scale/shear components) R_j, $j \in \{1, \ldots, n_c\}$, to be applied to n_c selected triangles of the input model. The Poisson-based editing scheme manipulates the mesh gradient field instead of directly deforming the spatial coordinates of a triangle mesh. By expressing the mesh in terms of the gradient operators G_j, for each triangle t_j, Poisson-based methods are able to derive a novel surface mesh $\mathcal{M}'_{tri}$ that matches the deformed gradient field subject to the user's constraints.

Gradient operators G_j contain the gradients of the triangle's shape functions ϕ_i and can be expressed by

$$
\begin{aligned}
G_j &= (\nabla\phi_1, \nabla\phi_2, \nabla\phi_3) \\
&= \begin{pmatrix} (p_1-p_3)^T \\ (p_2-p_3)^T \\ n^T \end{pmatrix}^{-1} \begin{pmatrix} 1 & 0 & -1 \\ 0 & 1 & -1 \\ 0 & 0 & 0 \end{pmatrix}
\end{aligned}
$$

Here p_j are the three vertices of the triangle t_j and n is its unit normal. The matrices G_j can be combined into a large $3m \times n$ gradient operator matrix G, and the gradients of the entire input triangle mesh then can be represented by

$$
Gp^x = g_x. \tag{3.1}
$$

The same holds true for the other two coordinate functions (g_y and g_z). By multiplying with $G^T M$ an both sides, we can rewrite Eq. 3.1 as follows

$$
G^T M G p^x = G^T M g_x, \tag{3.2}
$$

where the $3m \times 3m$ weight matrix M contains the areas of the triangles. The matrix $G^T M G$ is the cotangent discretization of the Laplace-Beltrami operator L_s [10, 20] and $\delta = G^T M g_x$ represents the differential coordinates of $\mathcal{M}_{tri}$.

This construction allows us to manipulate $\mathcal{M}_{tri}$ by applying the user constraints as separate transformations R_j to each δ_j, which yields $\delta'_j = \delta_j R_j$. At the end, we can reconstruct $\mathcal{M}'_{tri}$ in its new target configuration by computing the new vertex positions p' such that the resulting mesh complies with the new, rotated gradients. This can be computed by solving the Poisson system $L_s p' = \delta'$, which is formulated as a least-squares system for each x, y and z-coordinate separately.

Unfortunately, this formulation is only able to correctly reconstruct $\mathcal{M}'_{tri}$ if constraints are given for all triangles, i.e. such that we can transform all gradients. Alternatively, if only a sparse set of constraints is giving, the idea proposed in [36, 2] can be used to propagate the rotations over the whole model based on harmonic field interpolation.

After converting the input transformations R_j to unit quaternions, we regard each component of the quaternion $q = [q_x, q_y, q_z, q_w]$ as a scalar field defined over the entire mesh. A smooth interpolation is generated by regarding these scalar fields as harmonic fields defined over $\mathcal{M}_{tri}$, and can be computed efficiently by solving the Laplace equation ($L_s q = 0$) with constraints at the selected vertices. Once the rotational components (q_x, q_y, q_z and q_w) are computed for all vertices, we average the quaternion rotations of the vertices to obtain a quaternion rotation for each triangle. This way, we establish a geometric transformation R_j for each triangle t_j of $\mathcal{M}_{tri}$.

After estimating the rotations for all triangles, we perform the procedure described above to transform all gradients and obtain a realistic reconstruction of the model in a new pose. During the interactive editing process, the differential operator matrix L_s does not change. Furthermore, since it is symmetric positive definite, we can perform a sparse Cholesky decomposition as a preprocessing step and use back-substitution for each new set of input constraints R.

3.2.2 Guided Laplacian-Based Method

The input to this approach is a static triangle mesh $\mathcal{M}_{tri}$ and positional constraints $v_j \approx pc_j$, $j \in \{1,\ldots,n_c\}$ for selected n_c vertices of $\mathcal{M}_{tri}$. The Laplacian-based editing scheme represents the surface by the differential coordinates δ. The goal is to reconstruct the vertex positions of $\mathcal{M}'_{tri}$ such that the mesh approximates the initial differential coordinates δ, and the positional constraints given by the user.

Differential coordinates δ for $\mathcal{M}_{tri}$ are computed by solving a linear system of the form $\delta = L_s V_{tri}$, where L_s is the discrete Laplace operator based on the cotangent-weights [20]. Thereafter, the model $\mathcal{M}'_{tri}$ can be reconstructed in a new pose subject to the positional constraints pc by solving the following least-squares system:

$$\underset{V'_{tri}}{\operatorname{argmin}}\{\|L_s V'_{tri} - \delta\|^2 + \|A V'_{tri} - pc\|^2\}, \tag{3.3}$$

which can be transformed into a linear system

$$(L_s^T L_s + A^T A)V'_{tri} = L_s^T \delta + A^T pc. \tag{3.4}$$

In Eq. 3.4, pc is the vector of positional constraints specified by the user and the matrix A is a diagonal matrix containing non-zero weights $A_{ij} = w_j$ for constrained vertices v_j. The weights w_j indicate the influence of the corresponding positional constraint pc_j on the final deformation result.

Unfortunately, if the mesh undergoes large rotations, this scheme will reconstruct the mesh with an unnatural look, since most of the triangles will be oriented according to the original differential coordinates of $\mathcal{M}_{tri}$ [30]. However, the quality of the deformation result can be improved by carefully handling the local transformations of the differential coordinates [32, 1].

As in Sect. 3.2.1, after converting the input rotations R to quaternions, we interpolate the transformations q over $\mathcal{M}_{tri}$. Each component of the quaternion q is regarded as a scalar field defined on the entire mesh. A smooth interpolation is guaranteed by regarding these scalar fields as harmonic fields. The interpolation is performed efficiently by solving the Laplace equation $L_s q = 0$ over the entire mesh with constraints at the selected vertices.

Thereafter, we use the interpolated local transformations to rotate the differential coordinates, $\delta' = q \cdot \delta \cdot \bar{q}$. At the end, the vertex positions V'_{tri} of $\mathcal{M}'_{tri}$ are reconstructed such that the mesh approximates the rotated differential coordinates δ', as well as the positional constraints pc. Rewriting Eq. 3.4, we have the following linear system

$$(L_s^T L_s + A^T A)V'_{tri} = L_s^T \delta' + A^T pc. \tag{3.5}$$

During the mesh editing process, the Laplacian matrix L_s does not change. Therefore, we are able to perform a sparse matrix decomposition and execute only back-substitution for each new set of input constraints.

3.3 Iterative Volumetric Laplacian Approach

In contrast to the two previous methods, the iterative volumetric Laplacian method works on a tetrahedral mesh $\mathscr{T}_{tet} = (V_{tet}, T_{tet})$, with n_t vertices $V_{tet} = \{vt_1 \cdots vt_{n_t}\}$ and m_t tetrahedra $T_{tet} = \{tt_1 \cdots tt_{m_t}\}$. A tetrahedral mesh can, for instance, be created from a triangle mesh $\mathscr{M}_{tri}$ by performing a quadric error decimation on $\mathscr{M}_{tri}$ [13] and then building a face-constrained Delaunay tetrahedralization [28].

The input to this approach [31] is $\mathscr{T}_{tet}$ and positional constraints $pc_j, j \in \{1, \ldots, n_c\}$ for n_c selected vertices. This method infers rotational constraints from the given positional constraints and also improves the overall deformation performance by implicitly encoding stronger prior on the shape properties that should be preserved after the deformation, such as local cross-sectional areas.

It is our goal to deform the tetrahedral mesh $\mathscr{T}_{tet}$ as naturally as possible under the influence of a set of positional constraints $vt_j \approx pc_j, j \in \{1, \ldots, n_c\}$. To this end, we iterate a linear Laplacian deformation step and a subsequent update step, which compensates the (mainly rotational) errors introduced by the nature of the linear deformation. This algorithm is related to [29]. However, here a tetrahedral construction is used rather than a triangle mesh, as this enables the implicit preservation of certain shape properties, such as cross-sectional areas, after deformation.

The approach starts by constructing the tetrahedral Laplacian system $L_s V_{tet} = \delta$ with

$$L_s = G^T D G, \tag{3.6}$$

and

$$\delta = G^T D g, \tag{3.7}$$

where G is the discrete gradient operator matrix for the volumetric model, D is a $4m_t \times 4m_t$ diagonal matrix containing the tetrahedra's volumes, g is the set of tetrahedron gradients, each being calculated as $g_j = G_j p_j$ [10], and p_j is a matrix containing the vertex coordinates of tetrahedron tt_j. The constraints pc_j can be factorized into the matrix L_s by eliminating the corresponding rows and columns in the matrix and incorporating the values into the right-hand side δ.

By solving the previous tetrahedral Laplacian system, we obtain a set of new vertex positions $V'_{tet} = \{vt'_1 \ldots vt'_{n_t}\}$. After calculating a transformation matrix T_i which brings tt_i into configuration tt'_i, the matrix T_i is split into a rigid part R_i and a non-rigid part S_i using an iterative polar decomposition method [27]. Thereafter, only the rigid transformations are applied to the gradients of all respective tetrahedra in Eq. 3.7 and we rebuild the right-hand side of the linear system using these rotated gradients $g' = g \cdot R$. It is possible to pre-calculate a factorization of the left-hand side matrix once (since it never changes) and only perform an efficient back-substitution in each iteration.

During the iteration process we search for a new configuration of the input shape that minimizes the amount of non-rigid deformation S_i remaining in each tetrahedron. We refer to this deformation energy as $E_D = \sum_{i \in \mathcal{T}_{tet}} S_i$. In comparison with simulation methods such as [22, 8], this technique has the advantages of being extremely fast, of being very easy to implement, and of producing plausible results even if material properties are unknown.

Propagating the deformation from $\mathcal{T}_{tet}$ to $\mathcal{M}_{tri}$

After deforming $\mathcal{T}_{tet}$, we can transfer the pose from $\mathcal{T}'_{tet}$ to the input triangle mesh. Initially, we represent the vertices of $\mathcal{M}_{tri}$ as linear combinations of tetrahedra in the local neighborhood. To this end, for each vertex v_i in $\mathcal{M}_{tri}$, we find the subset $T_r(v_i)$ of all tetrahedra from $\mathcal{T}_{tet}$ that lie within a local spherical neighborhood of radius r and contain a boundary face with a face normal similar to that of v_i. Subsequently, we calculate the barycentric coordinate coefficients $c_i(j)$ of the vertex with respect to all $tt_j \in T_r(v_i)$ and compute the combined coefficient vector c_i as

$$c_i = \frac{\sum_{tt_j \in T_r(v_i)} c_i(j) \phi(v_i, tt_j)}{\sum_{tt_j \in T_r(v_i)} \phi(v_i, tt_j)} .$$

$\phi(v_i, tt_j)$ is a compactly supported radial basis function with respect to the distance of v_i to the barycenter of tetrahedron tt_j:

$$\phi(v_i, tt_j) = \begin{cases} 0 & \text{if } d > r \\ (1 - \frac{d}{r})^4 (\frac{4d}{r} + 1) & \text{if } d \leq r \end{cases}$$

$$\text{with } d = \|v_i - center(tt_j)\| .$$

The coefficients for all vertices of $\mathcal{M}_{tri}$ are combined into a matrix B. Thanks to the smooth partition of unity definition and the local support of our parameterization, we can quickly compute a smooth and natural looking deformed pose $\mathcal{M}'_{tri}$ by calculating the new vertex positions as $V'_{tri} = V'_{tet}B$.

References

1. de Aguiar, E., Theobalt, C., Stoll, C., Seidel, H.P.: Rapid animation of laser-scanned humans. In: IEEE Virtual Reality 2007, pp. 223–226 (2007)
2. de Aguiar, E., Zayer, R., Theobalt, C., Magnor, M., Seidel, H.P.: Video-driven animation of human body scans. In: IEEE 3DTV Conference (2007)
3. Alexa, M.: Local control for mesh morphing. In: Proc. of SMI 2001, p. 209 (2001)
4. Au, O.K.C., Fu, H., Tai, C.L., Cohen-Or, D.: Handle-aware isolines for scalable shape editing. In: ACM SIGGRAPH (2007)
5. Bechmann, D.: Space deformation models survey. Computers and Graphics 18(4), 571–586 (1994)
6. Botsch, M., Kobbelt, L.: An intuitive framework for real-time freeform modeling. In: Proc. ACM SIGGRAPH, pp. 630–634 (2004)

 7. Botsch, M., Pauly, M., Gross, M., Kobbelt, L.: Primo: Coupled prisms for intuitive sur-
    face modeling. In: Proc. SGP, pp. 11–20 (2006)
 8. Botsch, M., Pauly, M., Wicke, M., Gross, M.: Adaptive space deformations based on
    rigid cells. Computer Graphics Forum 26(3), 339–347 (2007)
 9. Botsch, M., Sorkine, O.: On linear variational surface deformation methods. IEEE
    TVCG 14(1), 213–230 (2008)
10. Botsch, M., Sumner, R., Pauly, M., Gross, M.: Deformation transfer for detail-preserving
    surface editing. In: Proc. VMV, pp. 357–364 (2006)
11. Fu, H., Au, O.K.C., Tai, C.L.: Effective derivation of similarity transformations for im-
    plicit laplacian mesh editing. Computer Graphics Forum 26(1), 34–45 (2007)
12. von Funck, W., Theisel, H., Seidel, H.P.: Vector field based shape deformations. In: Proc.
    ACM SIGGRAPH, pp. 1118–1125 (2006)
13. Garland, M., Heckbert, P.S.: Surface simplification using quadric error metrics. In: Proc.
    ACM SIGGRAPH, pp. 209–216 (1997)
14. Guskov, I., Sweldens, W., Schröder, P.: Multi-resolution signal processing for meshes.
    In: Proc. SIGGRAPH 1999, pp. 325–334 (1999)
15. Huang, J., Shi, X., Liu, X., Zhou, K., Wei, L.Y., Teng, S.H., Bao, H., Guo, B., Shum,
    H.Y.: Subspace gradient domain mesh deformation. ACM Trans. Graph. 25(3), 1126–
    1134 (2006)
16. Kobbelt, L., Campagna, S., Vorsatz, J., Seidel, H.P.: Interactive multi-resolution model-
    ing on arbitrary meshes. In: Proc. SIGGRAPH 1998, pp. 105–114 (1998)
17. Kraevoy, V., Sheffer, A.: Mean-value geometry encoding. International Journal of Shape
    Modeling, 29–46 (2006)
18. Lee, A., Moreton, H., Hoppe, H.: Displaced subdivision surfaces. In: Proc. SIGGRAPH
    2000, pp. 85–94 (2000)
19. Lipman, Y., Sorkine, O., Cohen-Or, D., Levin, D., Rössl, C., Seidel, H.P.: Differential
    coordinates for interactive mesh editing. In: Proc. of Shape Modeling International, pp.
    181–190 (2004)
20. Meyer, M., Desbrun, M., Schröder, P., Barr, A.H.: Discrete differential geometry op-
    erators for triangulated 2-manifolds. In: Visualization and Mathematics III, pp. 35–57
    (2003)
21. Milliron, T., Jensen, R.J., Barzel, R., Finkelstein, A.: A framework for geometric warps
    and deformations. ACM Trans. Graph. 21(1), 20–51 (2002)
22. Mueller, M., Dorsey, J., McMillan, L., Jagnow, R., Cutler, B.: Stable real-time deforma-
    tions. In: Proc. of SCA 2002, pp. 49–54 (2002)
23. Popa, T., Julius, D., Sheffer, A.: Material-aware mesh deformations. In: Proc. of SMI
    2006, p. 22 (2006)
24. Sederberg, T.W., Scott, R.P.: Free-form deformation of solid geometric models. In: Proc.
    ACM SIGGRAPH, pp. 151–160 (1986)
25. Sheffer, A., Kraevoy, V.: Pyramid coordinates for morphing and deformation. In: Proc.
    3D Data Processing, Visualization, and Transmission, pp. 68–75 (2004)
26. Shi, X., Zhou, K., Tong, Y., Desbrun, M., Bao, H., Guo, B.: Mesh puppetry: Cascad-
    ing optimization of mesh deformation with inverse kinematics. ACM SIGGRAPH 2007
    (2007)
27. Shoemake, K., Duff, T.: Matrix animation and polar decomposition. In: Proc. of Graphics
    Interface, pp. 258–264 (1992)
28. Si, H., Gaertner, K.: Meshing piecewise linear complexes by constrained delaunay tetra-
    hedralizations. In: Proc. International Meshing Roundtable, pp. 147–163 (2005)
29. Sorkine, O., Alexa, M.: As-rigid-as-possible surface modeling. In: Proc. SGP, pp. 109–
    116 (2007)

30. Sorkine, O., Lipman, Y., Cohen-Or, D., Alexa, M., Rössl, C., Seidel, H.P.: Laplacian surface editing. In: Proc. SGP, pp. 179–188 (2004)
31. Stoll, C., de Aguiar, E., Theobalt, C., Seidel, H.P.: A volumetric approach to interactive shape editing. Technical Report MPI-I-2007-4-004, MPII (2007)
32. Stoll, C., Karni, Z., Rössl, C., Yamauchi, H., Seidel, H.P.: Template deformation for point cloud fitting. In: Symposium on Point-Based Graphics, pp. 27–35 (2006)
33. Xu, W., Zhou, K., Yu, Y., Tan, Q., Peng, Q., Guo, B.: Gradient domain editing of deforming mesh sequences. ACM TOG 26(3), 84 (2007)
34. Yoshizawa, S., Belyaev, A.G., Seidel, H.P.: Free-form skeleton-driven mesh deformations. In: Proc. Symposium on Solid Modeling and Applications, pp. 247–253 (2003)
35. Yu, Y., Zhou, K., Xu, D., Shi, X., Bao, H., Guo, B., Shum, H.Y.: Mesh editing with poisson-based gradient field manipulation. In: Proc. ACM SIGGRAPH, pp. 644–651 (2004)
36. Zayer, R., Rössl, C., Karni, Z., Seidel, H.P.: Harmonic guidance for surface deformation. In: Proc. Eurographics, pp. 601–609 (2005)
37. Zhou, K., Huang, J., Snyder, J., Liu, X., Bao, H., Guo, B., Shum, H.Y.: Large mesh deformation using the volumetric graph laplacian. In: Proc. ACM SIGGRAPH, pp. 496–503 (2005)
38. Zorin, D., Schröder, P., Sweldens, W.: Interactive multiresolution mesh editing. In: Proc. SIGGRAPH 1997, pp. 259–268 (1997)

Chapter 4
Recording Studio: Data Acquisition and Data Processing

This chapter describes our recording studio. First, the physical studio, the camera system, and the full body laser scanner are presented. Thereafter, the acquisition pipeline is detailed, with all necessary steps to generate the input data for the projects described in this book.

It is a new trend in computer graphics to employ data acquired from the real world into the animation or rendering pipeline. For instance, the new research directions of performance capture and 3D Video investigate the possibility of generating realistic moving human models of real subjects from a set of images or video streams of the subject performing.

In this chapter, we extend the studio described in [30], which was originally designed for different surround vision applications. We present our new acquisition setup that provides high quality data for the different projects involving arbitrary subjects, motions, and clothing styles. Although our focus is different from previous work, the old functionality should be preserved, and augmented to meet the new requirements: high frame rates, high image resolution, better lighting conditions, and a device to reconstruct high-quality surface models for the subjects being recorded.

This chapter is structured as follows: Sect. 4.1 presents related acquisition systems for capturing multi-view video data. Thereafter, the details of the main components of our studio are presented, Sect. 4.2. At the end, in Sect. 4.3, all necessary recording steps to generate the data used in our projects are described, including camera calibration, recording session and data processing.

4.1 Related Acquisition Facilities

For video-based human motion capture, researchers use multiple video streams showing a moving person from different viewing directions to acquire the motion parameters. Commercial motion capture systems exist that use optical markers on the body in connection with several high-resolution special purpose cameras [21]. Examples of such commercial systems are provided by [1, 2, 24, 3, 4, 5].

E. de Aguiar: Animation & Performance Capture Using Digi. Models, COSMOS 5, pp. 29–36.
springerlink.com   © Springer-Verlag Berlin Heidelberg 2010

In contrast, marker-free motion capture systems do not require any intrusion into the scene. Examples of early motion capture acquisition systems are presented by [11, 17, 14] and [7, 18] using reconstructed volumes. Most recently, a system using a database of human shapes and fast high-resolution cameras was presented by [8]. A commercial marker-less motion capture system developed by Organic Motion^{TM} [27] is also available. Please refer to [25] for an extensive review of video-based motion capture systems.

Multi-view video streams can also be used for scene reconstruction. In this case, the viewer has the possibility to interactively choose the viewpoint of the dynamic 3D scene, while it is rendered [22]. A system for recording and editing 3D videos is described in [35] and further extended in [101]. Examples of other 3D Video systems are presented by [20, 28].

Alternatively, for reflectance acquisition systems, different acquisition setups consisting of high-quality cameras and a set of light sources have been proposed [33, 12]. [10] presented the *light stage* and most recently successively extended it, being able to acquire simple motion and dynamic reflectance fields of humans [6].

Most of the previous setups can acquire data for different and challenging tasks as motion capture, scene reconstruction and reflectance estimation. However, there is no system described in the literature yet that is able to provide high-resolution temporally-coherent virtual actors for arbitrary real-world subjects.

4.2 Recording Studio

Our studio is designed to acquire high-quality surface models of human subjects as well as image footage for measuring human motion, dynamic shape deformations, and appearance. In the following sections, we describe in details the requirements and solutions for each component of our studio: the studio room, the camera and lighting system, and the full body laser scanner.

4.2.1 Studio Room

The studio is installed in a room of approximately 9×4.8 meters in size. Its spatial dimensions are large enough to allow the scanning of subjects as well as recording of dynamic scenes from a large number of viewpoints. The ceiling has a height of approximately 4m. Along one of the shorter walls, an area of 2.5×4.8 meters is separated as a control room of the studio and for our full body laser scanner, Sect. 4.2.4. The walls and the floor can be covered with opaque black curtains and a carpet, respectively, which enables us to minimize the effects of indirect illumination in a scene. The recording area, the control room of our studio, and the laser scanner are shown in Fig. 4.1.

4.2.2 Camera System

The cameras used in the studio need to provide high frame-rates, high resolution, precise color reproduction, lossless data capture, and external synchronization,

Fig. 4.1 Our recording studio includes (a) the recording area, b the control room, and (c) the laser scanner.

which ensures that the multiple streams are correctly registered in time. Our camera system was ordered out-of-the box according to these specifications. The manufacturer [9] also provided us with a custom-made control software, Streams [29].

The system is composed of eight Imperx™ MDC1004 single chip CCD cameras that feature a 1004x1004 CCD sensor with linear 12 bits-per-pixel resolution, Fig. 4.2(a). The CCD uses a Bayer mosaic to record red, green, and blue channel information. The CCD sensor is connected to two controller chips. With both controllers activated, the camera provides a sustained frame rate of 48 fps at full resolution. However, in dual-mode the photometric responses of the sensors do not comply and an intra-frame color adjustment step is necessary. With only one chip activated, 25 fps at full resolution are feasible and no color balancing in the images is required.

The cameras are linked to a control PC equipped with 8 high-speed frame grabber boards. Each frame grabber is connected to a camera through a Camera Link™ interface. For maximal performance, each capture card is equipped with an on board SCSI interface enabling direct streaming of image data to a RAID system. Eight RAID systems are employed in parallel to enable real-time storage of the video streams. The synchronization is performed via a trigger pulse that is broadcasted to each capture card.

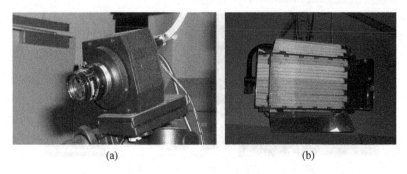

      (a)   (b)

Fig. 4.2 Equipments: **(a)** Camera and **(b)** softlight used in the studio.

The cameras can be installed at arbitrary locations in the studio. For positioning them, telescope poles (Manfrotto^{TM} Autopole [19]) with 3-degree-of-freedom mounting brackets (Manfrotto^{TM} Gear Head Junior [19]) are used that can be jammed between the floor and the ceiling. In general, the cameras are placed in an circular arrangement around the center of the scene and enable us to capture a volume of approximately $3.5 \times 3.5 \times 3$ meters.

4.2.3 Lighting System

The illumination of the studio is a fundamental issue for generating quality image footage. In our studio, the lighting conditions are fully controllable. For example, no exterior light can enter the recording area and the influence of indirect illumination is minimized by the black curtains and the carpet. Robust separation between foreground and background is also essential, i.e. the amount of shadows cast on the floor has to be minimized. Furthermore, the lighting system should produce a very uniform lighting, giving the scene a natural appearance.

In our studio, we employ a generic lighting configuration using 8 NesyFlex 440 DI ^{TM} compact softlights [23] that are optimized for universal use in TV and video studios, Fig. 4.2(b). Each light component contains 8 fluorescent day light tubes that radiate even light at an wide angle. They illuminate objects in the center of the scene from the top of the recording area and spread the light homogeneously downwards. The system can be controlled as a single unit using the DMX ^{TM} controls. Additionally, each light can be rotated to fulfill specific requirements. By this end, the lighting system prevents direct illumination into the camera lenses, which could lead to glares. The illumination system produces a uniform diffuse lighting in the scene, which avoids sharp shadows and unwanted highlights on the recorded subjects.

4.2.4 Full Body Laser Scanner

The geometric detail of the body of each recorded subject is captured by our Vitus Smart^{TM} full body laser scanner [32], Fig. 4.1(c). The device is compact, measuring

2.1 × 1.9 × 2.8 meters, and could be easily integrated in our studio. The scanner uses four columns which are mounted at an angle of approximately 90 degrees in relation with the subject to be scanned. Each column hosts an eye-safe laser scanner and two cameras that sit on a vertically moving gantry. The device employs a light-stripe method to collect high-speed 3D measurements. The final scan comprises of a 3D point cloud measured at an accuracy of 5 × 5 × 4 millimeters.

With a person standing on the scanner's platform, the scanning instruments start at the person's head and move down to scan the entire body. The scanning device is designed to handle different subjects and many different poses for a wide range of applications. It is able to scan a cylindrical volume of approximately 2.1 × 0.9 meters.

The whole scanning process takes approximately 11s and is controlled by a software running on a computer. This software, provided by Human Solutions [26], also gives the operator the possibility to perform some simple editing operations on the captured data.

4.3 Data Acquisition

Our recording studio efficiently acquires scanned models, camera attributes, and multi-view image footage to be used by the projects described in this book. Our acquisition pipeline can be divided into two stages: pre-recording and recording. In the first stage, all necessary information needed to calibrate the cameras and post-process the image data is captured. Afterwards, the actual recording session takes place, where the laser-scanned model and the multi-view image footage are acquired.

4.3.1 Pre-recording

In this stage, all necessary data required to post-process the multi-view video footage and to calibrate the cameras is collected. The following steps are performed:

- Camera calibration
- Color calibration
- Background subtraction

4.3.1.1 Camera Calibration

For our applications, the internal and external parameters of each of the 8 cameras have to be determined, Sect. 2.1. To this end, we first record two known objects to be used by our calibration algorithms: a smaller calibration pattern positioned in front of the camera, Fig. 4.3(a), and a large checkerboard positioned on the floor, Fig. 4.3(b).

We start by using the Heikkila's method [13] to calculate the intrinsic parameters and undistort the calibration images accordingly. This algorithm jointly estimates

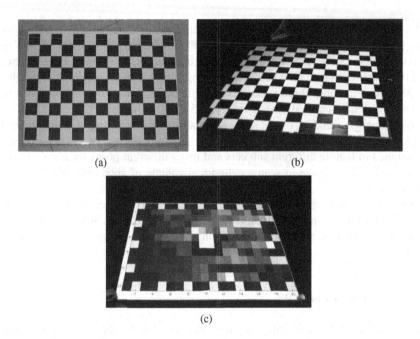

(a)   (b)

(c)

Fig. 4.3 Information acquired during the pre-recording session: (**a**) smaller calibration pattern used for intrinsic parameter estimation; (**b**) large checkerboard on the floor used for extrinsic parameter estimation; (**c**) color calibration pattern used for color adjustment.

intrinsic and extrinsic parameters from the images of our small calibration pattern and models the lens aberrations more accurately by considering radial and tangential lens distortions up to second order [16]. Afterwards, we also apply this information to correct and undistort each recorded camera stream.

Thereafter, using the undistorted images, we estimate the external parameters by means of the Tsai algorithm [31]. The corners of the checkerboard are automatically detected [15] and an optimization procedure determines the extrinsic parameters that minimize the reprojection error between the camera model's prediction of the pattern appearance and the actual images.

4.3.1.2 Color Calibration

Faithful color reproduction is ensured by white-balancing all cameras before the recording session. However, even after this step the color response of the cameras can be different, for example due to noise and slight physical differences in the built-in camera components. In order to assure color-consistency across the cameras, we record a large diffuse calibration pattern which consists of an array of 237 uniformly colored squares with purely lambertian reflectance, Fig. 4.3(c).

We use the recorded images of this color pattern to estimate for each camera a tri-linear transformation of the RGB color values in a least-squares sense. We typically perform relative photometric calibration. We define one camera to be the reference camera and for each remaining one, a color transformation is computed such that the color values of the pattern in the reference view are reproduced. At the end, color-consistency across the cameras is assured by applying this transformation to each recorded camera stream.

4.3.1.3   Background Subtraction

For the projects described in this book, the separation of the foreground subject from the background is essential. Our studio design already simplifies this process since the effects of external light on the scene and shadows cast on the walls are minimized. In order to segment the multi-view image data, we employ the algorithm described in Sect. 2.3.1 that robustly separates the moving human actor from the background. This algorithm computes mean color and standard deviation for each background pixel from a sequence of images without a foreground object, which is recorded prior to each human performance. By this means, foreground pixels can be identified by a large deviation of their color from the background statistics.

4.3.2   Recording

Our recording session consists of three steps. Before recording a set of performances, the data needed for camera calibration and post-processing is acquired: small and large checkerboard images, color pattern and background images. Then, for each subject, we acquire a triangle mesh model with our Vitus Smart™ full body laser scanner. Thereafter, the subject immediately moves to the nearby area where his/her performance is recorded by our eight synchronized video cameras.

In general, before recording each sequence, we ask the person to initially strike the same pose that he/she was scanned in. This simplifies the alignment process between scanned model and recorded images.

References

1. Ariel dynamics: Apas performance analysis system, http://www.arielnet.com
2. Motion analysis corporation: Eagle and hawk,
   http://www.motionanalysis.com
3. Qualisys: Oqus and proreflex, http://www.qualisys.com
4. Simi reality motion systems: Simi motion, http://www.simi.com
5. Vicon - vicon mx and vicon motus, http://www.vicon.com
6. Chabert, C.F., Einarsson, P., Jones, A., Lamond, B., Ma, W.C., Sylwan, S., Hawkins, T., Debevec, P.: Relighting human locomotion with flowed reflectance fields. In: ACM SIGGRAPH 2006 Sketches, p. 76 (2006)
7. Cheung, G., Kanade, T., Bouguet, J.Y., Holler, M.: A real time system for robust 3D voxel reconstruction of human motions. In: Proc. of CVPR, vol. 2, pp. 714–720 (2000)
8. Corazza, S., Mundermann, L., Chaudhari, A., Demattio, T., Cobelli, C., Andriacchi, T.: A markerless motion capture system to study musculoskeletal biomechanics: Visual hull and simulated annealing approach. Annals of Biomedical Engineering 34(11), 1019–1029 (2006)

9. Cosyco, http://www.cosyco.de
10. Debevec, P., Hawkins, T., Tchou, C., Duiker, H.P., Sarokin, W., Sagar, M.: Acquiring the reflectance field of a human face. In: ACM SIGGRAPH 2000, pp. 145–156 (2000)
11. Gavrila, D.M., Davis, L.S.: 3D model-based tracking of humans in action: A multi-view approach. In: Proc. of CVPR, pp. 73–80 (1996)
12. Goesele, M., Lensch, H., Heidrich, W., Seidel, H.P.: Building a photo studio for measurement purposes. In: Proc. of VMV 2000, pp. 231–238 (2000)
13. Heikkila, J., Silven, O.: Calibration procedure for short focal length off-the-shelf ccd cameras. In: Proc. of 13th ICPR, pp. 166–170 (1996)
14. Horprasert, T., Haritaoglu, I., Harwood, D., Davis, L., Wren, C., Pentland, A.: Real-time 3d motion capture. In: Second Workshop on Perceptual Interfaces, pp. 87–90 (1998)
15. Intel: Open source computer vision library (2002),
    http://www.sourceforge.net/projects/opencvlibrary
16. Jain, R., Kasturi, R., Schunck, B.G.: Machine Vision. McGraw Hill International, New York (1995)
17. Kanade, T., Saito, H., Vedula, S.: The 3d room: Digitizing time-varying 3d events by synchronized multiple video streams. Tech. Rep. CMU-RI-TR-98-34, Robotics Institute - Carnegie Mellon University (1998)
18. Luck, J., Small, D.: Real-time markerless motion tracking using linked kinematic chains. In: Proc. of CVPRIP (2002)
19. MANFROTTO, http://www.manfrotto.com
20. Matusik, W., Pfister, H.: 3d tv: a scalable system for real-time acquisition, transmission, and autostereoscopic display of dynamic scenes. In: ACM SIGGRAPH 2004, pp. 814–824 (2004)
21. Menache, A.: Understanding Motion Capture for Computer Animation and Video Games. Morgan Kaufmann, San Francisco (1995)
22. Narayanan, P.J., Rander, P., Kanade, T.: Constructing virtual worlds using dense stereo. In: Proc. of ICCV 1998, pp. 3–10 (1998)
23. Nesys, http://www.nesys.de/
24. PhaseSpace, http://www.phasespace.com
25. Poppe, R.: Vision-based human motion analysis: An overview. CVIU 108, 4–18 (2007)
26. Solutions, H., http://www.human-solutions.com/
27. Stage, O.M., http://www.organicmotion.com
28. Starck, J., Hilton, A.: Surface capture for performance based animation. IEEE CGAA 27(3), 21–31 (2007)
29. Streams, http://www.ioindustries.com
30. Theobalt, C., Li, M., Magnor, M., Seidel, H.P.: A flexible and versatile studio for synchronized multi-view video recording. In: Proc. of VVG, pp. 9–16 (2003)
31. Tsai, R.Y.: An efficient and accurate camera calibration technique for 3d machine vision. In: Proc. of CVPR, pp. 364–374 (1986)
32. Vitronic, http://www.vitronic.de/
33. Ward, G.J.: Measuring and modeling anisotropic reflection. In: Proc. of SIGGRAPH, pp. 265–272 (1992)
34. Waschbüsch, M., Würmlin, S., Cotting, D., Sadlo, F., Gross, M.: Scalable 3D video of dynamic scenes. In: Proc. PG, pp. 629–638 (2005)
35. Wuermlin, S., Lamboray, E., Staadt, O.G., Gross, M.H.: 3d video recorder: a system for recording and playing free-viewpoint video. Comput. Graph. Forum 22(2), 181–194 (2003)

Part II
Natural Animation of Digitized Models

Chapter 5
Problem Statement and Preliminaries

This part reviews the steps involved in the traditional skeleton-based character animation paradigm, and proposes two mesh-based alternatives that simplify the conventional process.

In recent years, photo-realistic computer-generated animations of humans have become the most important visual effect in motion pictures and computer games. In order to obtain an authentic virtual actor, it is of great importance that he/she mimics as closely as possible the motion of his/her real-world counterpart. Even the slightest unnaturalness would be instantaneously unmasked by the unforgiving eye of the viewer and the illusion of seeing a real person would be compromised.

In order to generate virtual people, animators make use of a well-established but often inflexible set of tools (see Sect. 5.1) that makes a high amount of manual interaction unavoidable. First, the geometry of the human body is hand-crafted in a modeling software or obtained from a laser scan of a real individual [7]. In a second step, a kinematic skeleton model is implanted into the body by means of, at best, a semi-automatic procedure [20]. In order to couple the skeleton with the surface mesh, an appropriate representation of pose-dependent skin deformation has to be found [25]. Finally, a description of body motion in terms of joint parameters of the skeleton is required. It can either be designed in a computer or learned from a real actor by means of motion capture [13, 27]. Although the interplay of all these steps delivers animations of stunning naturalness, the whole process is very labor-intensive and does not easily allow for the interchange of animation descriptions between different virtual subjects.

In this part of the book, we present two versatile, fast and simple alternatives that streamline the whole pipeline from laser-scanning to animation. Although our approaches abandon the concept of a kinematic skeleton, they integrate into the traditional animation workflow and enable animators to quickly produce convincing animation results with minimal manual labor, while still allowing for control over the production process.

The first approach, Chapter 6, is based on the Guided Poisson-based Deformation Method (Sect. 3.2.1) and the second one, Chapter 7, extends the first animation

E. de Aguiar: Animation & Performance Capture Using Digi. Models, COSMOS 5, pp. 39–43.
springerlink.com   © Springer-Verlag Berlin Heidelberg 2010

scheme by using the Guided Laplacian-based Deformation Method (Sect. 3.2.2). In general, both algorithms expect as input a geometric model (scanned or hand-crafted) in the form of a triangle mesh, and a description of the motion that the model should perform. As a result, they animate the input model generating convincing skinned body surfaces and also enabling simple motion retargeting, i.e. they enable the animator to interchange motions between persons of even widely different body proportions with no additional effort. Moreover, animations can be generated at interactive frame rates and the animators have instantaneous feedback when designing or modifying the animations. We demonstrate the performance of the proposed methods by using marker-based and marker-less motion capture data.

The main contributions of this part of the book is the

- integration of a Poisson-based and a Laplacian-based mesh deformation technique with a motion capture system to create an efficient and easy-to-use alternative to the traditional skeleton-based character animation pipeline [3, 4, 5],
- and the development of an intuitive animation tool providing full control over motion characteristics and deformation properties.

This chapter proceeds with a review of closely related work in Sect. 5.1. Afterwards, in Chapter 6 and 7, we describe the details of both mesh-based character animation methods.

5.1 Related Work

The first step in human character animation is the acquisition of a human body model comprising of a surface mesh and an underlying animation skeleton [11]. Surface geometry can either be hand-crafted or scanned from a real person [7].

The skeleton model can be either manually designed, inferred from marker trajectories [23, 2] or inferred from shape-from-silhouette volumes [1]. Similarly, kinematic skeletons can be reconstructed from a set of range scans of humans [8] or by fitting a template to body scans [9]. Recently, new methods are also able to extract plausible human animation skeletons from a static surface mesh of a character by using prior knowledge [10, 29].

Geometry and skeleton need to be connected such that the surface deforms realistically with the body motion. A popular method serving this purpose is vertex skinning [25] (see also Sect. 13.1). It represents position changes of individual vertices as a weighted set of transformations associated with adjacent joints. Deformation models can also be created by interpolating a set of scans [6], by combining a marker-based motion capture system with a shape-from silhouette method [28] or by capturing and animating surface deformations using a commercial motion capture system and approximately 350 markers [26].

The virtual human is animated by assigning motion parameters to the joints in the skeleton. Common methods to generate such motion descriptions are key-framing [14], physics-based animation [16] or optimization-based creation of physically plausible movements [17]. However, the most authentic motion representation is acquired through marker-based [13, 20] or marker-less motion capture systems [27]. Unfortunately, reusing motion capture data for subjects of different body proportions is not trivial, and requires computationally expensive motion editing [18, 24] and motion retargeting techniques [19, 33].

In general, most current work on character animation is focused on improving particular steps of the traditional pipeline such that animators can create realistic results efficiently. Only a small number of people has been working on methods to make the overall production process easier [12] and less dependent on the use of an underlying skeleton [22].

On the other hand, as highly detailed 3D triangle meshes become more and more accessible, there has been an increasing interest in devising techniques which can work directly on these geometric representations without requiring the overhead of intermediate pipelines such as the one mentioned above. The potential of mesh-based deformation techniques for character animation has already been stated in the literature. Using a complete set of correspondences between different synthetic models, [31] can transfer the motion of one model to the other one. Following a similar line of thinking, [32, 15] propose a mesh-based inverse kinematics framework based on pose examples. [30] presents a multi-grid technique for efficient deformation of large meshes and [21] presents a framework for performing constrained mesh deformation using gradient domain techniques. Most recently, [34] proposes a set of mesh-based operations to post-process mesh animations that unfortunately requires a fundamental redesign of existing animation tools.

In the following chapters, we present two methods that are able to simplify the traditional animation process [3, 4, 5]. Although they abandon the concept of a kinematic skeleton, the approaches integrate into the traditional animation workflow and enable animators to quickly produce convincing animation results. In contrast to related methods, they provide a complete integration with a motion acquisition system and provide an intuitive animation tool that gives full control over motion characteristics and deformation properties.

References

1. de Aguiar, E., Theobalt, C., Magnor, M., Theisel, H., Seidel, H.P.: M3: Marker-free model reconstruction and motion tracking from 3d voxel data. In: Proc. of PG, pp. 101–110 (2004)
2. de Aguiar, E., Theobalt, C., Seidel, H.P.: Automatic learning of articulated skeletons from 3d marker trajectories. In: Proc. ISVC, pp. 485–494 (2006)
3. de Aguiar, E., Theobalt, C., Stoll, C., Seidel, H.P.: Rapid animation of laser-scanned humans. In: IEEE Virtual Reality 2007, pp. 223–226 (2007)
4. de Aguiar, E., Zayer, R., Theobalt, C., Magnor, M., Seidel, H.P.: A simple framework for natural animation of digitized models. In: IEEE SIBGRAPI (2007)
5. de Aguiar, E., Zayer, R., Theobalt, C., Magnor, M., Seidel, H.P.: Video-driven animation of human body scans. In: IEEE 3DTV Conference (2007)
6. Allen, B., Curless, B., Popović, Z.: Articulated body deformation from range scan data. ACM Trans. Graph. 21(3), 612–619 (2002)
7. Allen, B., Curless, B., Popović, Z.: The space of human body shapes: Reconstruction and parameterization from range scans. ACM Trans. Graph. 22(3), 587–594 (2003)

8. Anguelov, D., Koller, D., Pang, H., Srinivasan, P., Thrun, S.: Recovering articulated object models from 3d range data. In: Proc. of UAI, pp. 18–26 (2004)
9. Anguelov, D., Srinivasan, P., Koller, D., Thrun, S., Rodgers, J., Davis, J.: Scape: Shape completion and animation of people. ACM Trans. Graph. 24(3), 408–416 (2005)
10. Aujay, G., Hétroy, F., Lazarus, F., Depraz, C.: Harmonic skeleton for realistic character animation. In: SCA 2007, pp. 151–160 (2007)
11. Badler, N., Metaxas, D., Magnenat-Thalmann, N.: Virtual Humans. Morgan Kaufmann, San Francisco (1999)
12. Baran, I., Popović, J.: Automatic rigging and animation of 3d characters. ACM Trans. Graph. 26(3), 72 (2007)
13. Bodenheimer, B., Rose, C., Rosenthal, S., Pella, J.: The process of motion capture: Dealing with the data. In: Computer Animation and Simulation 1997, pp. 3–18 (1997)
14. Davis, J., Agrawala, M., Chuang, E., Popović, Z., Salesin, D.: A sketching interface for articulated figure animation. In: Proc. of SCA 2003, pp. 320–328 (2003)
15. Der, K.G., Sumner, R.W., Popović, J.: Inverse kinematics for reduced deformable models. In: Proc. ACM SIGGRAPH, pp. 1174–1179 (2006)
16. Faloutsos, P., van de Panne, M., Terzopoulos, D.: The virtual stuntman: Dynamic characters with a repertoire of autonomous motor skills. Computers and Graphics 25(6), 933–953 (2001)
17. Fang, A.C., Pollard, N.S.: Efficient synthesis of physically valid human motion. ACM Trans. Graph. 22(3), 417–426 (2003)
18. Gleicher, M.: Motion editing with space-time constraints. In: Proc. of Symposium on Interactive 3D Graphics, pp (1997)
19. Gleicher, M.: Retargetting motion to new characters. In: Proc. of ACM SIGGRAPH, pp. 33–42 (1998)
20. Herda, L., Fua, P., Plänkers, R., Boulic, R., Thalmann, D.: Skeleton-based motion capture for robust reconstruction of human motion. In: CA 2000: Proc. of the Computer Animation (2000)
21. Huang, J., Shi, X., Liu, X., Zhou, K., Wei, L.Y., Teng, S.H., Bao, H., Guo, B., Shum, H.Y.: Subspace gradient domain mesh deformation. ACM Trans. Graph. 25(3), 1126–1134 (2006)
22. Igarashi, T., Moscovich, T., Hughes, J.F.: As-rigid-as-possible shape manipulation. In: SIGGRAPH 2005, pp. 1134–1141 (2005)
23. Kirk, A.G., O'Brien, J.F., Forsyth, D.A.: Skeletal parameter estimation from optical motion capture data. In: CVPR, pp. 782–788 (2005)
24. Lee, J., Shin, S.Y.: A hierarchical approach to interactive motion editing for human-like figures. In: Proc. of ACM SIGGRAPH, pp. 39–48 (1999)
25. Lewis, J.P., Cordner, M., Fong, N.: Pose space deformation: a unified approach to shape interpolation and skeleton-driven deformation. In: Proc. of ACM SIGGRAPH 2000, pp. 165–172 (2000)
26. Park, S.I., Hodgins, J.K.: Capturing and animating skin deformation in human motion. ACM Transactions on Graphics (SIGGRAPH 2006) 25(3), 881–889 (2006)
27. Poppe, R.: Vision-based human motion analysis: An overview. CVIU 108, 4–18 (2007)
28. Sand, P., McMillan, L., Popović, J.: Continuous capture of skin deformation. ACM Trans. Graph. 22(3), 578–586 (2003)
29. Schaefer, S., Yuksel, C.: Example-based skeleton extraction. In: SGP 2007, pp. 153–162 (2007)
30. Shi, L., Yu, Y., Bell, N., Feng, W.W.: A fast multigrid algorithm for mesh deformation. ACM Trans. Graph. 25(3), 1108–1117 (2006)

31. Sumner, R.W., Popović, J.: Deformation transfer for triangle meshes. In: Proc. ACM SIGGRAPH, pp. 399–405 (2004)
32. Sumner, R.W., Zwicker, M., Gotsman, C., Popović, J.: Mesh-based inverse kinematics. In: Proc. ACM SIGGRAPH, pp. 488–495 (2005)
33. Tak, S., Ko, H.S.: A physically-based motion retargeting filter. ACM Trans. Graph. 24(1), 98–117 (2005)
34. Xu, W., Zhou, K., Yu, Y., Tan, Q., Peng, Q., Guo, B.: Gradient domain editing of deforming mesh sequences. ACM TOG 26(3), 84 (2007)

Chapter 6
Poisson-Based Skeleton-Less Character Animation

This chapter presents an approach to efficiently generate high-quality animations of human characters from input motion data. Using a Poisson-based deformation method, as described in Sect. 3.2.1, the proposed approach outputs character animations with realistic body deformations, only requiring a minimum of manual interaction.

In order to generate photo-realistic animations of humans, animators make use of a well-established but often inflexible set of tools that makes a high amount of manual interaction unavoidable, Sect. 5.1. In this chapter, we describe a versatile, fast and simple mesh-based alternative to animate human models that completely integrates into the traditional animation workflow.

Our approach can be used to realistically animate models of humans without relying on kinematic skeletons, which reduces the animator's effort to a great extent. Furthermore, it produces realistic pose-dependent body deformations and it solves the motion transfer problem, i.e. it enables the animator to interchange motions between persons of even widely different body proportions with no additional effort.

The main contributions of this chapter are

- the integration of a Poisson-based mesh deformation technique with a motion capture system to create an efficient and simple alternative to the conventional character animation pipeline [1, 2], and
- the development of an intuitive animation tool providing full control over motion characteristics and deformation properties.

This chapter proceeds with an overview of our algorithm in Sect. 6.1, and the description of our simple interface prototype in Sect. 6.2. Thereafter, we demonstrate that we can realistically animate human models using marker-based and marker-less motion capture data, Sect. 6.3. Finally, results and conclusions are presented in Sect. 6.4.

6.1 Overview

Our goal is to provide animators with a simple and fast method to directly apply captured motion to human models, e. g. scanned models. The input to our method

E. de Aguiar: Animation & Performance Capture Using Digi. Models, COSMOS 5, pp. 45–54.
springerlink.com

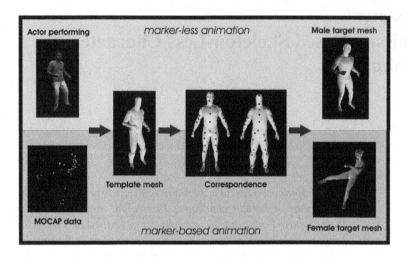

Fig. 6.1 Illustration of the workflow of our system.

is a human body scan $\mathcal{M}_{tri}$ and motion data generated from real individuals using optical motion estimation methods, Fig. 6.1. The first processing step normalizes these sequences of key body poses by transforming them into a sequence of postures of a simple triangle mesh model, henceforth termed *template mesh*. In Sect. 6.3.1 and 6.3.2 we exemplify that it is straightforward to generate such templates from motion capture data.

By regarding motion transfer as a pure deformation problem, we can put aside all difficulties related to the dissimilarities between the template and the input model, as anatomical disparities or body proportions, and take advantage of their semantic similarities, e.g. the fact that both mesh representations have knees and elbows. To this end, we ask the user to specify a set of *correspondence triangles* between the template and $\mathcal{M}_{tri}$.

The motion of the template mesh from a reference pose, as shown in Fig 6.2(a), into another pose (Fig 6.2(c)) is captured by the deformation of a small set of triangles marked under the guidance of the user. Applying these deformations to the corresponding triangles of $\mathcal{M}_{tri}$ brings it from its own reference pose, as shown in Fig 6.2(b), into the deformed template's pose, Fig 6.2(d). For this purpose, we first align template and input models in a given reference pose. By subsequently applying the motion transfer procedure to all input frames, the motion from the moving template mesh is correctly transfered to the input high-quality body model.

6.2 Prototype Interface

Our method does not require skeleton information or full correspondence between the template and the input model. The motion transfer process is controlled by the set of markers chosen by the user. We decided to resort to this interactive step since

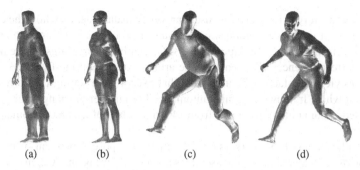

(a)   (b)   (c)   (d)

Fig. 6.2 A template model (**a**) and a high-resolution body scan (**b**) in their respective reference poses. The template in a pose obtained via motion capture (**c**) and its pose transferred to the human scan (**d**). Reprinted from [2] © 2007 IEEE.

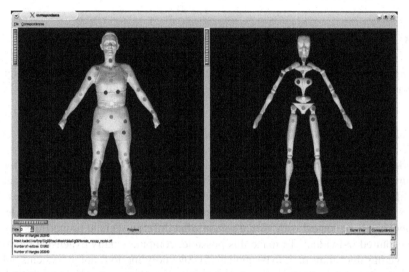

Fig. 6.3 Prototype interface used in our system, featuring easy selection of correspondences and instantaneous feedback. Reprinted from [1] © 2007 IEEE.

there is no viable automatic approach that can identify body segments on meshes standing in general poses.

Our easy and intuitive prototype interface allows access to both models at their reference poses simultaneously, Fig. 6.3. An automatic alignment of the models is performed upon loading the mesh files. When a triangle is selected on one model, a corresponding triangle on the other one is highlighted. The artist can decide to keep this correspondence or improve it manually. For cylindrically shaped body parts, we require the user to specify a single correspondence triangle and we mark additional triangles automatically by taking additional directions in the cross-sectional plane and intersecting them with the mesh. For geometrically more complex body parts, such as the lap or the shoulders, correspondences need to be specified by the user.

Using our prototype interface, the user can verify instantaneously how the correspondences will influence the deformation transfer process. By loading a template mesh in a deformed pose, the input model $\mathcal{M}_{tri}$ can be deformed using the actual selected correspondences. This enables the artist to decide on-the-fly if the correspondences yield satisfactory results. Note that except from setting the correspondences, our whole framework is fully automatic. The number of triangle correspondences used in our animations ranges from 140 to 220, half of which is automatically generated.

As the placement of the markers directly affects the pose-dependent surface deformation of the scanned mesh, the user does not have to tweak any weights as in the commonly used skinning methods. The principle here is simple: for having a sharp bend in the surface, the correspondences should be placed close to either side of the joint, Fig. 6.4 (left). Increasing the distance of the markers from the joint allows for a softer bending, Fig. 6.4 (right).

6.3   Animating Human Scans Using Motion Capture Data

Using motion capture data as the front-end to our framework, we create two intriguing applications: mesh-based character animation and video-driven animation.

6.3.1   Mesh-Based Character Animation

Marker-based tracking systems [3] provide the animator with motion descriptions of unequaled accuracy and naturalness. Even subtle details in motion patterns are faithfully captured. However, the high quality of the captured motion data comes at the expense of many inflexibilities in their application. Firstly, motion parameters cannot easily be reused with virtual persons that differ in skeletal proportions from the captured individual. To make this possible, computationally expensive motion retargeting algorithms have to be applied [5]. Secondly, motion capture systems only deliver a description of human motion in terms of interconnected rigid bodies. The non-rigid deformations of the skin and the soft-tissue surrounding the bones usually have to be manually modeled, e.g. by means of vertex skinning [6].

Our approach is able to simplify this process by directly animating human body scans with motion capture data. Paradoxically, despite discarding the use of a kinematic skeleton, it allows us to generate high-quality animations. The steps that have to be taken to animate the input scan are very simple: first, using any standard animation software, like 3D Studio Max™, the input motion data, as shown in Fig. 6.5(a), is transformed into a surface model in which the bones of the biped are represented as triangle meshes, Fig. 6.5(b). Consequently, using our prototype interface, static per-triangle correspondences between the triangulated biped and the input scanned mesh are defined. Finally, the Guided Poisson-based mesh deformation approach, as described in 3.2.1, realistically deforms the scanned model $\mathcal{M}_{tri}$, mimicking the motion of the animated template, Fig. 6.5(c).

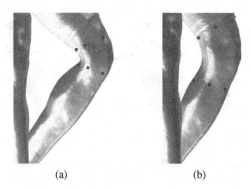

(a)   (b)

Fig. 6.4 Influence of the markers' placement on the deformation quality: marking correspondence triangles (red dots) close to an (anatomical) joint creates a sharp bend in the skin (**left**), while increasing the distance to the joint enables smoother bending (**right**). Reprinted from [1] © 2007 IEEE.

In order to use the deformation approach, the local transformations to be applied to the selected triangles of $\mathcal{M}_{tri}$ need to be estimated. This is done by calculating the transformation matrix R_i that brings the triangle t_i^{REF} at the reference frame into the configuration t_i^t at frame t, i.e. using the Jacobian. Using as input $\mathcal{M}_{tri}$ and the estimated transformations R, the deformation method is able to transfer the pose of the template to the scanned model. At the end, since the deformation approach is insensitive to translation, we also apply a global translation to $\mathcal{M}_{tri}'$ to bring it to the same location as the template model at the current frame.

We have applied our method to animate a male and a female scanned model. Input motion capture data are taken from a database of motion files provided by Eyes,

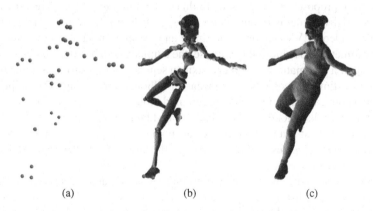

(a)   (b)   (c)

Fig. 6.5 The set of input markers (**a**) are used to generate an intermediate biped model using any standard animation software (**b**). By applying the Guided Poisson-based deformation technique, the acquired motion is realistically transferred to the input human body scan (**c**). Reprinted from [1] © 2007 IEEE.

Fig. 6.6 Subsequent frames generated by our system showing the female scan authentically performing a soccer kick. Note the realistic protrusion of the chest when she blocks the ball, as well as the original head motion. Reprinted from [1] © 2007 IEEE.

Japan Co. Ltd. Fig. 6.6 shows several frames of an animation in which we made the female model perform a soccer kick. The input is a motion capture file comprising of 90 key body poses. The actress realistically blocks the ball, kicks it and scores. Note that the animation nicely displays even subtle details like the protrusion of the chest during blocking. The skin deformation around the knees and the elbows is also authentically reproduced. Fig. 6.7 shows the male model performing boxing punches and jumping. Note that despite the fact that the input motions stem from persons with totally different anatomical dimensions, very natural animations are generated.

6.3.2   Video-Driven Animation

For non-intrusively estimating motion parameters, the passive optical motion capture approach proposed in [4] is used. To this end, a moving subject is recorded by eight static video cameras in our studio, Chapter 4. From the frame-synchronized multi-view video (MVV) streams, the shape and the motion parameters of the human are estimated. To achieve this purpose, the template model shown in Fig. 6.2(a), comprising of a kinematic skeleton and sixteen separate closed surface segments, is fitted to each time step of video by means of silhouette-matching. The output of the method conveniently represents the captured motion as a sequence in which the template model subsequently strikes the estimated body poses.

This output format can be directly used as input to our pipeline. First, the animator specifies triangle correspondences between the template and the scanned model $\mathscr{M}_{tri}$ at their reference poses. Thereafter, the mesh deformation scheme (Sect. 3.2.1) makes the human scan mimic the motion that we have captured in video. As in Sect. 6.3.1, local transformations R are calculated based on the deformation of the selected triangles of the template model between the reference and the current frame. The deformation method transfers the pose of the template to the scanned mesh, and at the end, a global translation is applied to $\mathscr{M}'_{tri}$ bringing it to the same position as the template model at the current frame.

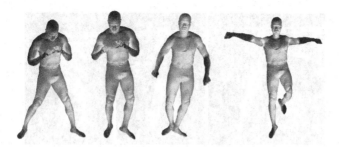

Fig. 6.7 Male model boxing (**left**) and jumping (**right**). Note the realistic skin deformation of the animated scanned model. Reprinted from [1] © 2007 IEEE.

We demonstrate the performance of our video-driven animation system by animating a female and a male scan with two different captured motion sequences. The first sequence contains 156 frames and shows a female subject performing a capoeira move. The second sequence is 330 frames long and shows a dancing male subject. Fig. 6.8 shows a comparison between actual input video frames and human scans striking similar poses. It illustrates that body poses recorded on video can be faithfully transferred to models of arbitrary human subjects. Differences in body shape and skeletal proportions can be neglected. These results also demonstrate that our method provides animators with a tool to conveniently transfer motion extracted from normal video streams onto human scans.

6.4 Results and Discussion

To demonstrate the potential of our framework, we conducted several experiments with both marker-based and marker-less motion acquisition techniques. Since for this project we did not have access to a full body laser scanner, we used the Cyberware models provided with their original surface colors in most of our experiments: a female model (264KΔ) and a male model (294KΔ). As shown in Fig. 6.6 and Fig. 6.7, the models faithfully reproduce the acquired performances of professional athletes. Marker-less motion acquisition enables us to perform video-driven animation. Both of our models in Fig. 6.8 authentically mimic the human performances captured on video.

The results confirm that our method is capable of delivering visually convincing character animation at a low interaction cost. The method is able to process large data sets in the order of 200 to 300 KΔ in just seconds. For smaller models of 30 to 50 KΔ, the results are generated at 2-5 frames per second. All the experiments were conducted on a single 3.2GHz notebook.

Our method can be seen as an enhancement to the artist's traditional animation workflow. In order to evaluate its performance, we conducted several experiments asking unexperienced users to animate a character using both our animation framework and a traditional animation software. A comparison of the resulting animations is shown in Fig. 6.9. This further confirms that our system is able to generate results

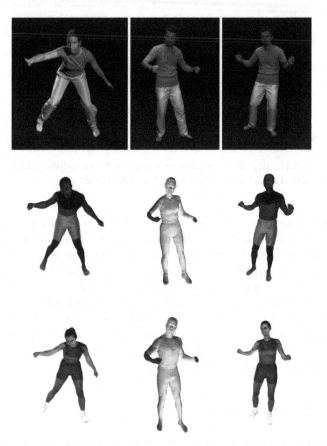

Fig. 6.8 Video-driven animation. Motion parameters are extracted from raw video footage of human performances (top row). By this means, body poses of a video-taped individual can easily be mapped to body scans of other human subjects (bottom rows). Reprinted from [2] © 2007 IEEE.

comparable to professional animation packages, like Character Studio ^{TM}, without requiring much effort. In the traditional animation pipeline, an unexperienced user needs many hours to correctly adjust the skinning weights. However, in our system, he/she is able to specify the correspondences quickly thanks to our prototype interface. After less than one hour, the animations shown in Fig. 6.9(b) can be produced. In fact, specifying correspondences is more intuitive to the user than working on building envelopes during the skinning process. In addition, correspondences can be tested instantaneously on our system, giving the user an adequate feedback.

As for any novel technique, our method still has some limitations. While our current system can handle different motion capture data as input, it does not provide intuitive key-framing capabilities. For extreme deformations, we also note that there is generally some loss in volume due to the nature of our mesh deformation tech-

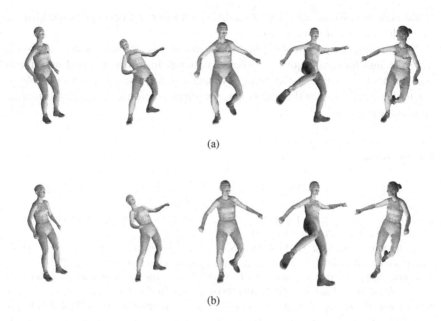

(a)

(b)

Fig. 6.9 Direct comparison between a character animation generated by an animation software package (**a**) and our system (**b**). Our method is able to provide the same visual quality, while requiring less effort and time from unexperienced users. Reprinted from [1] © 2007 IEEE.

nique, Sect. 3.2.1. Another limitation is that our system can not enforce positional constraints. Although it is not possible to explicitly enforce positional constraints, they can be implicitly specified by increasing the number of correspondences associated with a triangle or a region. For instance, we can ensure stable feet placement simply by marking a sufficient number of constraints on the feet. While allowing for an easy and intuitive control over the animation result, a wrong placement of correspondences can lead to unsatisfactory animation results, in the same way as bad skinning weights do in the classical animation pipeline. However, during our experiments, we could verify that bad correspondences can easily be detected and corrected using the instantaneous feedback provided by our prototype interface. On the other hand, correcting problems in the traditional animation pipeline needs a big amount of time and experience.

Most recently, a variety of mesh deformation techniques have been described in the literature, Sect. 3.1. The majority of these methods are conceptually related to our algorithm and could also be used to enhance the animation quality and the speed of our system. In the next chapter, we improve the performance of our animation framework by using a Laplacian-based mesh deformation scheme (Sect. 3.2.2) instead of a Poisson-based technique. This solves the translation insensibility problem of the current system, enabling the specification of positional constraints. Moreover, it allows the user to generate animations using a smaller number of correspondences, thus reducing the animator's effort.

Nonetheless, the proposed method is a step towards simplifying the traditional, not so straightforward acquisition-to-animation pipeline. It is easy and intuitive to use, and does not require any training. By means of the same efficient methodology, it simultaneously solves the animation, the surface deformation, and the motion retargeting problem.

References

1. de Aguiar, E., Zayer, R., Theobalt, C., Magnor, M., Seidel, H.P.: A simple framework for natural animation of digitized models. In: IEEE SIBGRAPI (2007)
2. de Aguiar, E., Zayer, R., Theobalt, C., Magnor, M., Seidel, H.P.: Video-driven animation of human body scans. In: IEEE 3DTV Conference (2007)
3. Bodenheimer, B., Rose, C., Rosenthal, S., Pella, J.: The process of motion capture: Dealing with the data. In: Computer Animation and Simulation 1997, pp. 3–18 (1997)
4. Carranza, J., Theobalt, C., Magnor, M., Seidel, H.P.: Free-viewpoint video of human actors. ACM TOG (Proc. of SIGGRAPH 2003) 22(3), 569–577 (2003)
5. Gleicher, M.: Retargetting motion to new characters. In: Proc. of ACM SIGGRAPH, pp. 33–42 (1998)
6. Lewis, J.P., Cordner, M., Fong, N.: Pose space deformation: a unified approach to shape interpolation and skeleton-driven deformation. In: Proc. of ACM SIGGRAPH 2000, pp. 165–172 (2000)

Chapter 7
Laplacian-Based Skeleton-Less Character Animation

This chapter extends the original mesh-based animation framework described in the previous chapter. By using a Laplacian-based scheme to guide the mesh deformation process, the improved system described here allows for more accurate control producing animations from motion capture data.

In the previous chapter, we introduced a versatile, fast and simple approach to animate characters from motion capture data. It uses a purely mesh-based animation paradigm that realistically animates static meshes of arbitrary humans without relying on kinematic skeletons. However, the previous approach does not allow the animator to specify positional constraints. Although they can be implicitly enforced by increasing the number of correspondences associated with a triangle, the lack of positional constraints makes it hard to produce an animation, as the user needs to specify more correspondences.

In this chapter, we extend the previous approach by employing a Laplacian-based technique, as described in Sect. 3.2.2, to guide the motion transfer process. As a result, our system is able to animate the human character taking into account rotational and positional constraints set by the user. This enhances the performance of the method, and makes it more robust against retargeting artifacts, e.g. feet sliding on the floor.

The main contribution of this chapter is the

- integration of a Laplacian-based mesh deformation technique with a motion capture system to create a simpler alternative to the traditional character animation pipeline [1].

The remainder of this chapter is structured as follows: Sect. 7.1 presents an overview of our improved animation framework. Applications of our method using both marker-based and marker-less motion capture data are shown in Sect. 7.2. Finally, results and conclusions are presented in Sect. 7.3.

E. de Aguiar: Animation & Performance Capture Using Digi. Models, COSMOS 5, pp. 55–61.
springerlink.com
© Springer-Verlag Berlin Heidelberg 2010

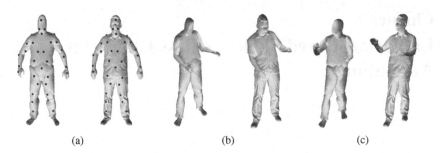

(a)   (b)   (c)

Fig. 7.1 (**a**) Template (used for marker-less data) and human models at their reference poses. Colored spheres represent corresponding selected vertices. (**b-c**) Models in different poses. Note how the human model is accurately deformed, mimicking the template model's pose. Reprinted from [1] © 2007 IEEE.

7.1 Overview

As in Chapter 6, inputs to this method are a scanned mesh $\mathcal{M}_{tri}$ and a description of the motion that the model should perform. To apply our framework, an input motion description has to be converted into a moving template model, which can either be a template triangle mesh or a template point cloud. After roughly aligning template and scanned models at their reference poses, a small set of corresponding vertices between the template and $\mathcal{M}_{tri}$ are specified. Thereafter, our Laplacian-based mesh deformation technique is used to efficiently transfer the motion of the template model to $\mathcal{M}_{tri}$. The deformation method generates animations at interactive frame rates, creates convincingly skinned body surfaces, and allows for simple motion retargeting.

Through placement of markers, the characteristics of the motion, the surface skinning, and the retargeting constraints are defined. Our graphical user interface, adapted from Sect. 6.2, assists the animator in controlling marker placement. A typical session consists of the following steps: first the user selects a vertex in the template model. Since template and input model have been roughly aligned, the system proposes a corresponding closest target vertex. Fortunately, we can compute deformed mesh poses at interactive rates, and thus a new pose $\mathcal{M}'_{tri}$ is shown instantaneously after setting each pairwise correspondence. Due to the immediate visual feedback, it is easy for the user to interactively modify correspondences.

As the corresponding vertices will drive the Laplacian-based deformation method, it is important that their choice captures as much as possible of the geometric deformation. The principle to place the markers is simple: they should be specified in areas where deformations are expected to happen, e.g. near anatomical joints. In addition, they can be specified in regions where the animator wants to enforce detailed deformation, for example in the torso, or explicit positional constraints. With the assistance of our interactive application, even unexperienced users quickly get a feeling of how to place markers. Each of the animations presented in Sect. 7.3 were generated in less than 15 minutes. Typically, between 35 to 65 markers are sufficient to create realistic animations.

Fig. 7.2 Several frames showing the input human model performing soccer moves. The input motion was captured by means of a marker-based optical motion capture system. Note the lifelike non-rigid surface deformations automatically generated. Reprinted from [1] © 2007 IEEE.

7.2 Animating Human Scans with Motion Capture Data

7.2.1 Mesh-Based Character Animation

Nowadays, skeletal motion data acquired with a marker-based optical system is widely-used in animation production. It is thus one of our main motivations to develop a method to easily apply these data to high-quality surface models, while bypassing the drawbacks of the traditional skeletal animation. Nearly all motion capture systems output a kinematic skeleton and a sequence of joint parameters. As stated in Sect. 6.3.1, we first automatically transform this kinematic representation into a moving template model using a standard animation software, like 3D Studio MAX^{TM}. Note that we do not generate another surface model, and that there are no requirements at all concerning shape and connectivity of the template, apart from it containing moving vertices.

Once the mesh template has been generated, local transformations R are calculated from the rotation of the selected vertices of the template between its reference pose and its pose at time t, by means of a graph-based method. To this end, the selected vertices on the template are considered nodes in a graph, and edges between them are determined by constructing the extended minimal spanning tree [3]. For each selected vertex, a local frame is generated by looking at its neighboring edges. A local rotation for each vertex is estimated from the change of the local frame between reference time and time t, i.e. using the Jacobian. These rotations are then assigned to the corresponding vertices of $\mathcal{M}_{tri}$. Positional constraints pc are derived

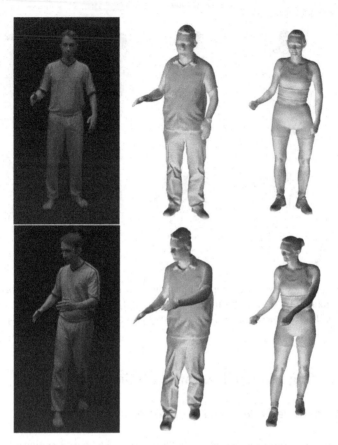

Fig. 7.3 Video-driven animation. Two comparisons between an input video frame and two models striking the same pose. Although the models have different body dimension with respect to the real human subject, the poses are reconstructed accurately. Reprinted from [1] © 2007 IEEE.

from the positions of the selected vertices of the template mesh at time t, and assigned to the corresponding vertices of $\mathcal{M}_{tri}$. Using as inputs $\mathcal{M}_{tri}$, R and pc, the Guided Laplacian-based approach is applied to animate the scanned human model over time.

We can even use the raw marker-trajectories output by the motion capture system as input to our method, as opposed to in Chapter 6. However, please note that the best positions of markers on the body for our purpose are different from the best marker positions for skeletal motion estimation. Obviously, most publicly available sequences have been captured with the latter application in mind, which makes it necessary to build a template prior to feeding them to our algorithm.

We have animated several laser-scanned subjects with motion files provided by Eyes Japan Co. Ltd. We generated convincingly moving characters, examples of which are shown in Fig. 7.2. Motion retargeting is achieved by appropriately placing constraints. With synthetic data, we could also verify that raw marker trajectories are a feasible input motion description.

7.2.2 Video-Driven Animation

Instead of explicitly-placed markings on the body, marker-less systems employ image features to estimate motion parameters from video. Similar to Sect. 6.3.2, using a silhouette-based marker-less motion capture system [2], the actor's motion parameters are measured, using a template body model comprising a segmented surface mesh and an underlying skeleton, from 8 multi-view video streams.

Since a mesh template is already used for tracking, we can employ the deformation scheme to straightforwardly map the captured motion to scans of other persons. As in Sect. 7.2.1, positional constraints pc are assigned to vertices of $\mathcal{M}_{tri}$ from the corresponding vertices of the template mesh at time t. Rotational constraints R are derived from the movement of the selected markers of the template from the reference frame to the current frame. By applying these constraints to the Guided Laplacian-based approach, the scanned human model is animated over time. Fig. 7.3 shows screenshots of animations that are obtained by mapping non-intrusively captured human performances to laser-scans of different subjects.

7.3 Results and Discussion

The animated body meshes of male and female subjects, captured with a Cyberware full-body scanner, exemplify the performance of our improved method. In the marker-based setting, we generated results from 10 different motion sequences, showing a variety of motions ranging from simple walking to soccer moves. The sequences were typically between 100 and 300 frames long. Fig. 7.2 shows several frames of different animations where the male model performs soccer moves. The human model realistically performs the motion, while exhibiting lifelike non-rigid surface deformations. Note that the fact that the scanned model has different dimensions compared to the recorded human subject is not a problem for our algorithm.

Marker-less animation examples are shown in Fig. 7.3 and Fig. 7.4. Fig. 7.3 shows a comparison between actual input video frames and two models striking similar poses. It illustrates that our method can accurately transfer poses captured on video to virtual characters. Fig. 7.4 shows some frames of a captured dancing sequence (330 frames) being mapped into a male model.

The quality of the results confirms that our animation framework is able to simplify the traditional, not so straightforward skeletal acquisition-to-animation pipeline. The framework described in this chapter is simple, versatile and enables us to compute target poses for $\mathcal{M}_{tri}$ at an interactive frame rate of 5 fps for models comprising of $10K\Delta$ to $30K\Delta$. As in Chapter 6, this approach also requires manual interaction. However, the main advantage over the previous one is the addition of positional constraints. This allows the user to animate a character using less correspondences and makes the system more robust against retargeting artifacts. Moreover, the improved framework does not require a sequence of template models and

Fig. 7.4 Example of a simple virtual environment using the male model. Some frames of the animated dancing sequence, captured from the performance of a real actor, are shown. Reprinted from [1] © 2007 IEEE.

it is able to create character animations using only the raw marker positions. By this means, animation production is simplified even further, as animations can be generated interactively during the motion capture process.

Our current method still presents some limitations regarding loss in volume during extreme deformations. However, this can be corrected by using advanced surface or volumetric mesh deformation methods as shown in [4, 5, 6]. Nonetheless, in this part of the book we describe an efficient methodology to directly animate characters from motion data, simultaneously solving the animation, the surface deformation, and the motion retargeting problem.

References

1. de Aguiar, E., Theobalt, C., Stoll, C., Seidel, H.P.: Rapid animation of laser-scanned humans. In: IEEE Virtual Reality 2007, pp. 223–226 (2007)
2. Carranza, J., Theobalt, C., Magnor, M., Seidel, H.P.: Free-viewpoint video of human actors. ACM TOG (Proc. of SIGGRAPH 2003) 22(3), 569–577 (2003)

3. Kruskal, J.B.: On the shortest spanning subtree of a graph and the traveling salesman problem. Proc. of the American Mathematical Society 7, 48–50 (1956)
4. Shi, L., Yu, Y., Bell, N., Feng, W.W.: A fast multigrid algorithm for mesh deformation. ACM Trans. Graph. 25(3), 1108–1117 (2006)
5. Sorkine, O., Alexa, M.: As-rigid-as-possible surface modeling. In: Proc. SGP, pp. 109–116 (2007)
6. Stoll, C., de Aguiar, E., Theobalt, C., Seidel, H.P.: A volumetric approach to interactive shape editing. In: Technical Report MPI-I-2007-4-004, MPII (2007)

Part III
Towards Performance Capture Using Deformable Mesh Tracking

Chapter 8
Problem Statement and Preliminaries

This part of the book first reviews the most relevant work on motion capture, scene reconstruction, and 3D Video. Thereafter, it describes three algorithms to passively capture the performance of human actors, and presents a system to generate high-quality 3D Videos.

Nowadays, stepping directly from a captured real-world sequence to the corresponding realistic moving character is still challenging. Since marker-based and marker-free motion capture systems measure the motion in terms of a kinematic skeleton, they have to be combined with other scanning technologies to capture the time-varying shape of the human body surface [12, 83, 72]. However, dealing with people wearing arbitrary clothing from only video streams is still not possible. In this part of the book, we propose three solutions to bridge this gap, enabling the direct animation of a high-quality static human scan from unaltered video footage. The algorithms presented in this part of the book jointly capture motion and time-varying shape detail even of people wearing wide apparel, while preserving a spatio-temporally coherent geometry over time. By being completely passive, they also enable us to record the subject's appearance, which can then be used to display the recorded actor from arbitrary viewpoints.

The proposed methods achieve a high level of flexibility and versatility by explicitly abandoning any traditional skeletal motion parameterization, and by posing *performance capture* as deformation capture. As a result, they produce a rich dynamic scene representation that can be easily made available to and modified by animators, which enables new applications in motion capture, computer animation and 3D Video.

To summarize, this part of the book presents the following contributions:

- a method to fully-automatically capture motion and time-varying deformation of people by combining optical flow and a fast Laplacian-based tracking scheme [11];
- a simple and robust method to automatically identify and track features on a moving arbitrary subject over time [10];
- an efficient approach to directly and realistically animate a static body scan from sparse marker trajectories [10];

E. de Aguiar: Animation & Performance Capture Using Digi. Models, COSMOS 5, pp. 65–73.
springerlink.com   © Springer-Verlag Berlin Heidelberg 2010

- a dense performance capture technique that reconstructs motion, time-varying geometry, and texture of actors performing fast and complex motions [7];
- a system to render high-quality 3D Videos of captured human performances [7].

This chapter proceeds with a review of closely related work in Sect. 8.1. Thereafter, in Chapters 9, 10, and 11, we describe the details of three performance capture methods. Finally, Chapter 12 presents a system to generate high-quality 3D Videos.

8.1 Related Work

We define *performance capture* as the full process of passively recording motion, dynamic geometry, and dynamic surface appearance of actors from multi-view video. Therefore, the work presented in this part of the book jointly solves a variety of algorithmic subproblems, and extends previous work in the fields of human motion capture, dynamic scene reconstruction, and 3D Video.

8.1.1 Human Motion Capture

Optical motion capture systems are the workhorses in many game and movie production companies for measuring motion of real performers [18]. Optical markings, which are either made of a retroreflective material or LEDs are placed on the body of a tracked subject and several high-frame-rate cameras are used to record the moving person. The locations of the markers in the video streams are tracked and their 3D trajectories over time are reconstructed by means of optical triangulation [5]. Thereafter, a kinematic skeleton is matched to the marker trajectories to parameterize the captured motion in terms of joint angles [50]. Although many commercial marker-based capturing systems are available, e.g. [1, 2, 74, 3, 4, 5], that deliver highly accurate motion data, the application of marker-based systems is still time-consuming, see Chapter 5. Furthermore, the captured individuals typically have to wear special body suits, and the use of markers does not allow the video streams to be employed for further processing, e.g. texture reconstruction.

Marker-less motion capture approaches are designed to overcome some restrictions of marker-based techniques and enable performance recording without optical scene modification [67, 68, 76]. A kinematic body model, typically consisting of a linked kinematic chain of bones and interconnecting joints, can be combined with a simple geometric primitive to model the physical outline of the human subject, enabling its motion estimation. Primitives like cylinders [88], stick figures [56], patches [53], cones [45], boxes [63], scaled prismatics [26], ellipsoids [30, 65] and superquadrics [43, 52, 90] can be used. Implicit surface models based on metaballs are also feasible [75]. Recently, more realistic models based on polygon meshes [25, 91, 64] and high-resolution scanned models [31, 15, 42] have also been employed.

In [71], an analysis-by-synthesis framework has been proposed that searches the space of possible body configurations, synthesizes model poses, and compares them to features in the image plane. By this means, the misalignment between these features, such as silhouettes [75, 25, 8], and the corresponding features of the projected model, drives a pose estimation and refinement process [54, 59, 46]. Another category of approaches uses optical flow constraints [22, 23], appearance models [98, 14], edges [90, 36], textured-models [41], depth constraints [32], inverse kinematics [106] and conformal geometric algebra [80] to drive the pose estimation procedure. Alternatively, divide and conquer methods using silhouettes [66], constraint propagation methods [27], and physics-based approaches [51, 34] have also been developed.

In contrast to the methods based on local [25, 29, 78, 70] or global [31] optimization, recently, the application of filtering approaches in the context of human motion capture has become very popular. If the model dynamics can be described by a linear model, a Kalman Filter can be used for tracking [73, 21, 65]. Assuming a non-linear dynamic model and Gaussian noise, particle filter approaches can be also employed [35, 88, 58, 37, 87, 100, 105]. Moreover, the combination of optimization and filtering techniques for tracking sophisticated 3D body models has also been demonstrated in several other publications [90, 20].

Recent systems are also based on learning approaches, where additional prior knowledge is taken into account during human motion estimation. This includes the use of prior poses or patterns from a motion database [88, 97, 79], tracking-by-detection approaches [84, 57, 69], or approaches that learn a map between image and pose spaces [47, 6, 55, 89].

Alternatively, instead of working with image features, kinematic body models can be fitted to dynamic 3D scene models that are reconstructed from multiple silhouette views [95, 28, 9].

8.1.2 Dynamic Scene Reconstruction

Motion capture systems [18, 50] take into account the subject's underlying kinematic structure to simplify the motion estimation process. However, the use of a skeleton structure restricts such methods to capture only articulated rigid body motions. Non-rigid surface deformations due to apparel or skin are not captured. Some approaches have been described in the literature aiming at solving this problem by using hundreds of optical markings [72], by jointly using a motion capture system and laser range scans of humans [12, 13] or by jointly employing a marker-based motion capture method and multi-view silhouette matching [83]. Although these approaches produce highly detailed deformable bodies, their commitment to a marker-based motion capture system makes it hard to use them for applications where interference in the scene is not allowed, e.g. 3D Video. Another limitation is the use of a priori knowledge about the subject, which makes generalization to animals or other objects difficult.

Marker-less motion capture approaches [76] are more flexible than intrusive methods. However, it is still difficult for them to achieve the same level of accuracy and the same application range. Furthermore, since most approaches employ kinematic body models, they cannot capture the motion and detailed shape of people in loose everyday apparel. Some methods try to capture more detailed body deformations, in addition to skeletal joint parameters, by adapting the models closer to the observed silhouettes [83, 15] or by jointly using silhouettes and cast shadows [16]. However, these algorithms require the subjects to wear tight clothes. Only few approaches, such as the work by [81], aim at capturing humans wearing more general attire, e.g. by jointly relying on kinematic body and cloth models.

Alternatively, shape-from-silhouette algorithms [44], multi-view stereo approaches [107], methods combining silhouette and stereo constraints [39, 40], and data-driven techniques [102, 38] can be used to reconstruct dynamic scene geometry. To obtain good quality results, however, many cameras are needed and it is hard for these algorithms to generate connectivity-preserving dynamic mesh models [92].

Some passive deformable model tracking methods extract 3D correspondences from images to track simple deformable objects [33], cloth [77], and surface deformations of tightly dressed humans [75, 8]. Statistical models have also shown their potential to track confined deformable surface patches [96] and moving hands [49]. Researchers have also used physics-based shape models to track garment [82] or simple articulated humans [73, 62, 24]. Unfortunately, none of these methods is able to track arbitrarily dressed people completely passively. It may also be difficult to apply them for tracking a human wearing different garments, since the specification of material parameters is non-trivial.

Recently, new animation design [19], animation editing [104], animation capture methods [17], and approaches to deform mesh-models into active scanner data [94] or visual hulls [85] have been developed. In another line of research, methods that jointly perform model generation and deformation capture from scanner data [99] have also been proposed. All these methods are no longer based on skeletal shape and motion parameterizations, but rely on surface models and general shape deformation approaches. Similar to these previous approaches, the performance capture methods proposed in this book follow this research direction. Although the explicit abandonment of kinematic parameterizations makes performance capture a harder problem, it bears the striking advantage that it enables capturing both rigidly and non-rigidly deforming surfaces with the same underlying technology.

8.1.3 3D Video

Research in 3D Video, or free-viewpoint video, aims at developing methods for photo-realistic, real-time rendering of previously captured real-world scenes. The goal is to give the user the freedom to interactively reconstruct real-world scenes from new synthetic camera views never seen by any real camera.

Early research that paved the way for free-viewpoint video was presented in the field of image-based rendering [86]. Shape-from-silhouette methods reconstruct rather coarse approximate 3D video geometry by intersecting multi-view silhouette cones. Examples are image-based [61, 103] or polyhedral visual hull methods [60], as well as approaches performing point-based reconstruction [48].

Despite their computational efficiency, the moderate quality of the textured coarse scene reconstructions often falls short of production standards in the movie and game industry. To boost 3D video quality, researchers experimented with multi-view stereo [107], multi-view stereo with active illumination [101], combinations of stereo and shape-from-silhouette [93], or model-based free-viewpoint video capture [25, 8]. However, the first three categories of approaches do not deliver spatio-temporally coherent geometry or 360 degree shape models, which are both essential prerequisites for animation post-processing. At the same time, it is extremely challenging for previous kinematic model-based techniques to capture performers in general clothing.

In contrast, by combining the captured detailed dynamic scene representations with a projective texture method, a system to render high-quality 3D Videos is designed, Chapter 12, enabling convincing renditions of human subjects from arbitrary synthetic viewpoints.

References

1. Ariel dynamics: Apas performance analysis system, http://www.arielnet.com
2. Motion analysis corporation: Eagle and hawk, http://www.motionanalysis.com
3. Qualisys: Oqus and proreflex, http://www.qualisys.com
4. Simi reality motion systems: Simi motion, http://www.simi.com
5. Vicon - vicon mx and vicon motus, http://www.vicon.com
6. Agarwal, A., Triggs, B.: Recovering 3d human pose from monocular images. IEEE PAMI 28(1), 44–58 (2006)
7. de Aguiar, E., Stoll, C., Theobalt, C., Ahmed, N., Seidel, H.P., Thrun, S.: Performance capture from sparse multi-view video. In: ACM TOG, Proc. SIGGRAPH (2008)
8. de Aguiar, E., Theobalt, C., Magnor, M., Seidel, H.P.: Reconstructing human shape and motion from multi-view video. In: CVMP 2005, pp. 42–49 (2005)
9. de Aguiar, E., Theobalt, C., Magnor, M., Theisel, H., Seidel, H.P.: M3: Marker-free model reconstruction and motion tracking from 3d voxel data. In: Proc. of PG, pp. 101–110 (2004)
10. de Aguiar, E., Theobalt, C., Stoll, C., Seidel, H.: Marker-less 3d feature tracking for mesh-based human motion capture. In: Proc. ICCV HUM 2007, pp. 1–15 (2007)
11. de Aguiar, E., Theobalt, C., Stoll, C., Seidel, H.P.: Marker-less deformable mesh tracking for human shape and motion capture. In: Proc. CVPR (2007)
12. Allen, B., Curless, B., Popović, Z.: Articulated body deformation from range scan data. ACM Trans. Graph. 21(3), 612–619 (2002)
13. Anguelov, D., Srinivasan, P., Koller, D., Thrun, S., Rodgers, J., Davis, J.: Scape: Shape completion and animation of people. ACM Trans. Graph. 24(3), 408–416 (2005)
14. Balan, A., Black, M.: An adaptive appearance model approach for model-based articulated object tracking. In: Proc. of CVPR, pp. 758–765 (2006)
15. Balan, A., Sigal, L., Black, M., Davis, J.E., Haussecker, H.W.: Detailed human shape and pose from images. In: Proc. CVPR (2007)
16. Balan, A., Sigal, L., Black, M., Haussecker, H.: Shining a light on human pose: On shadows, shading and the estimation of pose and shape. In: Proc. ICCV (2007)
17. Bickel, B., Botsch, M., Angst, R., Matusik, W., Otaduy, M., Pfister, H., Gross, M.: Multi-scale capture of facial geometry and motion. In: Proc. of SIGGRAPH (2007)
18. Bodenheimer, B., Rose, C., Rosenthal, S., Pella, J.: The process of motion capture: Dealing with the data. In: Computer Animation and Simulation 1997, pp. 3–18 (1997)

19. Botsch, M., Sorkine, O.: On linear variational surface deformation methods. IEEE TVCG 14(1), 213–230 (2008)
20. Bray, M., Koller-Meier, E., Gool, L.V.: Smart particle filtering for high-dimensional tracking. Comput. Vis. Image Underst. 106(1), 116–129 (2007)
21. Bregler, C.: Learning and recognizing human dynamics in video sequences. In: Proc. of CVPR 1997, p. 568 (1997)
22. Bregler, C., Malik, J.: Tracking people with twists and exponential maps. In: Proc. of CVPR 1998, pp. 8–15 (1998)
23. Brox, T., Rosenhahn, B., Cremers, D., Seidel, H.-P.: High accuracy optical flow serves 3-D pose tracking: Exploiting contour and flow based constraints. In: Leonardis, A., Bischof, H., Pinz, A. (eds.) ECCV 2006. LNCS, vol. 3952, pp. 98–111. Springer, Heidelberg (2006)
24. Brubaker, M.A., Fleet, D.J., Hertzmann, A.: Physics-based person tracking using simplified lower-body dynamics. In: Proc. CVPR (2007)
25. Carranza, J., Theobalt, C., Magnor, M., Seidel, H.P.: Free-viewpoint video of human actors. ACM TOG (Proc. of SIGGRAPH 2003) 22(3), 569–577 (2003)
26. Cham, T.J., Rehg, J.M.: A multiple hypothesis approach to figure tracking. In: Proc. of CVPR, pp. 2239–2245 (1999)
27. Chen, Z., Lee, H.: Knowledge-guided visual perception of 3d human gait from a single image sequence. IEEE Transactions on Systems, Man and Cybernetics 22(2), 336–342 (1992)
28. Cheung, G., Baker, S., Kanada, T.: Shape-from-silhouette of articulated objects and its use for human body kinematics estimation and motion capture. In: Proc. of CVPR, pp. 77–84 (2003)
29. Cheung, G., Baker, S., Kanade, T.: Shape-from-silhouette across time part ii: Applications to human modeling and markerless motion tracking. Int. J. Comput. Vision 63(3), 225–245 (2005)
30. Cheung, G., Kanade, T., Bouguet, J.Y., Holler, M.: A real time system for robust 3D voxel reconstruction of human motions. In: Proc. of CVPR, vol. 2, pp. 714–720 (2000)
31. Corazza, S., Mundermann, L., Chaudhari, A., Demattio, T., Cobelli, C., Andriacchi, T.: A markerless motion capture system to study musculoskeletal biomechanics: Visual hull and simulated annealing approach. Annals of Biomedical Engineering 34(11), 1019–1029 (2006)
32. Covelle, M.M., Rahimi, A., Harville, M., Darrell, T.J.: Articulated pose estimation using brighness and depth constancy constraints. In: Proc. of CVPR, vol. 2, pp. 438–445 (2000)
33. Decarlo, D., Metaxas, D.: Optical flow constraints on deformable models with applications to face tracking. IJCV 38(2), 99–127 (2000)
34. Delamarre, Q., Faugeras, O.: 3D articulated models and multi-view tracking with silhouettes. In: ICCV 1999, pp. 716–721 (1999)
35. Deutscher, B., Blake, A., Reid, I.: Articulated body motion capture by annealed particle filtering. In: Proc. of CVPR 2000, vol. 2, pp. 126–133 (2000)
36. Deutscher, J., Reid, I.: Articulated body motion capture by stochastic search. Int. J. Comput. Vision 61(2), 185–205 (2005)
37. Drummond, T., Cipolla, R.: Real-time tracking of highly articulated structures in the presence of noisy measurements. In: Proc. of ICCV, vol. 2, pp. 315–320 (2001)
38. Einarsson, P., Chabert, C.F., Jones, A., Ma, W.C., Lamond, B., Hawkins, T., Bolas, M., Sylwan, S., Debevec, P.: Relighting human locomotion with flowed reflectance fields. In: Proc. EGSR, pp. 183–194 (2006)
39. Esteban, C.H., Schmitt, F.: Silhouette and stereo fusion for 3d object modeling. CVIU 96(3), 367–392 (2004)

40. Furukawa, Y., Ponce, J.: Carved visual hulls for image-based modeling. In: Leonardis, A., Bischof, H., Pinz, A. (eds.) ECCV 2006. LNCS, vol. 3951, pp. 564–577. Springer, Heidelberg (2006)

41. Gall, J., Rosenhahn, B., Seidel, H.-P.: Robust pose estimation with 3D textured models. In: Chang, L.-W., Lie, W.-N. (eds.) PSIVT 2006. LNCS, vol. 4319, pp. 84–95. Springer, Heidelberg (2006)

42. Gall, J., Rosenhahn, B., Seidel, H.P.: Drift-free tracking of rigid and articulated objects. In: Proc. of CVPR (2008)

43. Gavrila, D.M., Davis, L.S.: 3D model-based tracking of humans in action: A multi-view approach. In: Proc. of CVPR, pp. 73–80 (1996)

44. Goldluecke, B., Magnor, M.: Space-time isosurface evolution for temporally coherent 3d reconstruction. In: Proc. CVPR, vol. I, pp. 350–355 (2004)

45. Goncalves, L., Di Bernardo, E., Ursella, E., Perona, P.: Monocular tracking of the human arm in 3D. In: Proc. of CVPR, pp. 764–770 (1995)

46. Grammalidis, N., Goussis, G., Troufakos, G., Strintzis, M.G.: Estimating body animation parameters from depth images using analysis by synthesis. In: Proc. of DCV 2001, p. 93 (2001)

47. Grauman, K., Shakhnarovich, G., Darrell, T.: Inferring 3d structure with a statistical image-based shape model. In: Proc. of ICCV 2003, p. 641 (2003)

48. Gross, M., Würmlin, S., Näf, M., Lamboray, E., Spagno, C., Kunz, A., Koller-Meier, E., Svoboda, T., Gool, L.V., Lang, S., Strehlke, K., Moere, A.V., Staadt, O.: Blue-c: a spatially immersive display and 3d video portal for telepresence. ACM TOG 22(3), 819–827 (2003)

49. Heap, T., Hogg, D.: Towards 3d hand tracking using a deformable model. In: FG 1996 (1996)

50. Herda, L., Fua, P., Plänkers, R., Boulic, R., Thalmann, D.: Skeleton-based motion capture for robust reconstruction of human motion. In: CA 2000: Proc. of the Computer Animation, p. 77 (2000)

51. Kakadiaris, I.A., Metaxas, D.: 3D human body model acquisition from multiple views. In: Proc. of ICCV 1995, pp. 618–623 (1995)

52. Kakadiaris, I.A., Metaxas, D.: Model-based estimation of 3D human motion with occlusion based on active multi-viewpoint selection. In: Proc. CVPR, pp. 81–87 (1996)

53. Kameda, Y., Minoh, M., Ikeda, K.: Three dimensional pose estimation of an articulated object from its silhouette image. In: Proc. of ACCV 1993, pp. 612–615 (1993)

54. Koch, R.: Dynamic 3D scene analysis through synthesis feedback control. PAMI 15(6), 556–568 (1993)

55. Lee, C.S., Elgammal, A.: Modeling view and posture manifolds for tracking. In: Proc. of ICCV 2007 (2007)

56. Lee, H.J., Chen, Z.: Determination of 3d human body postures from a single view 30(2), 148–168 (1985)

57. Loy, G., Eriksson, M., Sullivan, J., Carlsson, S.: Monocular 3d reconstruction of human motion in long action sequences. In: Pajdla, T., Matas, J(G.) (eds.) ECCV 2004. LNCS, vol. 3024, pp. 442–455. Springer, Heidelberg (2004)

58. MacCormick, J., Isard, M.: Partitioned sampling, articulated objects, and interface-quality hand tracking. In: Vernon, D. (ed.) ECCV 2000. LNCS, vol. 1843, pp. 3–19. Springer, Heidelberg (2000)

59. Martinez, G.: 3D motion estimation of articulated objects for object-based analysis-synthesis coding (OBASC). In: VLBV 1995, pp. 175–199 (1995)

60. Matsuyama, T., Takai, T.: Generation, visualization, and editing of 3D video. In: Proc. of 3DPVT 2002, p. 234 (2002)

61. Matusik, W., Buehler, C., Raskar, R., Gortler, S.J., McMillan, L.: Image-based visual hulls. In: Proc. SIGGRAPH, pp. 369–374 (2000)

62. Metaxas, D., Terzopoulos, D.: Shape and nonrigid motion estimation through physics-based synthesis. IEEE PAMI 15(6), 580–591 (1993)

63. Meyer, D., Denzler, J.: Model based extraction of articulated objects in image sequences for gait analysis. In: Proc. of ICIP 1997, p. 78 (1997)

64. Mikić, I., Trivedi, M., Hunter, E., Cosman, P.: Human body model acquisition and tracking using voxel data. Int. J. Comput. Vision 53(3), 199–223 (2003)

65. Mikić, I., Triverdi, M., Hunter, E., Cosman, P.: Articulated body posture estimation from multicamera voxel data. In: Proc. of CVPR, vol. 1, p. 455 (2001)

66. Mittal, A., Zhao, L., Davism, L.S.: Human body pose estimation using silhouette shape analysis. In: Proc. of AVSS, p. 263 (2003)

67. Moeslund, T.B., Granum, E.: A survey of computer vision-based human motion capture. CVIU 81(3), 231–268 (2001)

68. Moeslund, T.B., Hilton, A., Krüger, V.: A survey of advances in vision-based human motion capture and analysis. Comput. Vis. Image Underst. 104(2), 90–126 (2006)

69. Mori, G., Malik, J.: Recovering 3d human body configurations using shape contexts. IEEE PAMI 28(7), 1052–1062 (2006)

70. Mündermann, L., Corazza, S., Andriacchi, T.P.: Accurately measuring human movement using articulated icp with soft-joint constraints and a repository of articulated models. In: Proc. of CVPR (2007)

71. O'Rourke, J., Badler, N.I.: Model-based image analysis of human motion using constraint propagation. PAMI 2(6), 522–536 (1980)

72. Park, S.I., Hodgins, J.K.: Capturing and animating skin deformation in human motion. ACM Transactions on Graphics (SIGGRAPH 2006) 25(3), 881–889 (2006)

73. Pentland, A., Horowitz, B.: Recovery of nonrigid motion and structure. IEEE PAMI 13(7), 730–742 (1991)

74. PhaseSpace, http://www.phasespace.com

75. Plänkers, R., Fua, P.: Articulated soft objects for multiview shape and motion capture. IEEE PAMI 25(9), 1182–1187 (2003)

76. Poppe, R.: Vision-based human motion analysis: An overview. CVIU 108, 4–18 (2007)

77. Pritchard, D., Heidrich, W.: Cloth motion capture. In: Eurographics, pp. 263–271 (2003)

78. Rosenhahn, B., Brox, T., Kersting, U., Smith, D., Gurney, J., Klette, R.: A system for marker-less human motion estimation. Kuenstliche Intelligenz (KI) 1, 45–51 (2006)

79. Rosenhahn, B., Brox, T., Seidel, H.P.: Scaled motion dynamics for markerless motion capture. In: Proc. CVPR (2007)

80. Rosenhahn, B., Brox, T., Weickert, J.: Three-dimensional shape knowledge for joint image segmentation and pose tracking. In: IJCV, pp. 243–262 (2006)

81. Rosenhahn, B., Kersting, U., Powel, K., Seidel, H.P.: Cloth x-ray: Mocap of people wearing textiles. In: Franke, K., Müller, K.-R., Nickolay, B., Schäfer, R. (eds.) DAGM 2006. LNCS, vol. 4174, pp. 495–504. Springer, Heidelberg (2006)

82. Salzmann, M., Ilic, S., Fua, P.: Physically valid shape parameterization for monocular 3-d deformable surface tracking. In: BMVC (2005)

83. Sand, P., McMillan, L., Popović, J.: Continuous capture of skin deformation. ACM Trans. Graph. 22(3), 578–586 (2003)

84. Shakhnarovich, G., Viola, P., Darrell, T.: Fast pose estimation with parameter-sensitive hashing. In: Proc. of ECCV 2003, pp. 750–757 (2003)

85. Shinya, M.: Unifying measured point sequences of deforming objects. In: Proc. of 3DPVT, pp. 904–911 (2004)

86. Shum, H.Y., Chan, S.C., Kang, S.B.: Image-based rendering. Springer, Heidelberg (2007)
87. Sidenbladh, H., Black, M.J., Sigal, L.: Implicit probabilistic models of human motion for synthesis and tracking. In: Heyden, A., Sparr, G., Nielsen, M., Johansen, P. (eds.) ECCV 2002. LNCS, vol. 2350, pp. 784–800. Springer, Heidelberg (2002)
88. Sidenbladh, H., Black, M.J., Fleet, D.J.: Stochastic tracking of 3D human figures using 2D image motion. In: Vernon, D. (ed.) ECCV 2000. LNCS, vol. 1843, pp. 702–718. Springer, Heidelberg (2000)
89. Sminchisescu, C., Kanaujia, A., Metaxas, D.N.: Bm3e: Discriminative density propagation for visual tracking. IEEE PAMI 29(11), 2030–2044 (2007)
90. Sminchisescu, C., Triggs, B.: Kinematic jump processes for monocular 3d human tracking. In: Proc.of IEEE CVPR, pp. 69–76 (2003)
91. Starck, J., Hilton, A.: Model-based multiple view reconstruction of people. In: Proc. of ICCV, p. 915 (2003)
92. Starck, J., Hilton, A.: Spherical matching for temporal correspondence of non-rigid surfaces. In: IEEE ICCV, pp. 1387–1394 (2005)
93. Starck, J., Hilton, A.: Surface capture for performance based animation. IEEE CGAA 27(3), 21–31 (2007)
94. Stoll, C., Karni, Z., Rössl, C., Yamauchi, H., Seidel, H.P.: Template deformation for point cloud fitting. In: Symposium on Point-Based Graphics, pp. 27–35 (2006)
95. Theobalt, C., Magnor, M., Schüler, P., Seidel, H.P.: Combining 2d feature tracking and volume reconstruction for online video-based human motion capture. In: Proc. PG, pp. 96–103 (2002)
96. Torresani, L., Hertzmann, A.: Automatic non-rigid 3D modeling from video. In: Pajdla, T., Matas, J(G.) (eds.) ECCV 2004. LNCS, vol. 3022, pp. 299–312. Springer, Heidelberg (2004)
97. Urtasun, R., Fua, P.: 3D human body tracking using deterministic temporal motion models. In: Pajdla, T., Matas, J(G.) (eds.) ECCV 2004. LNCS, vol. 3023, pp. 92–106. Springer, Heidelberg (2004)
98. Vacchetti, L., Lepetit, V., Fua, P.: Stable real-time 3d tracking using online and offline information. IEEE Trans. Pattern Anal. Mach. Intell. 26(10), 1385–1391 (2004)
99. Wand, M., Jenke, P., Huang, Q., Bokeloh, M., Guibas, L., Schilling, A.: Reconstruction of deforming geometry from time-varying point clouds. In: Proc. SGP, pp. 49–58 (2007)
100. Wang, P., Rehg, J.M.: A modular approach to the analysis and evaluation of particle filters for figure tracking. In: Proc. CVPR 2006, pp. 790–797 (2006)
101. Waschbüsch, M., Würmlin, S., Cotting, D., Sadlo, F., Gross, M.: Scalable 3D video of dynamic scenes. In: Proc. PG, pp. 629–638 (2005)
102. Wilburn, B., Joshi, N., Vaish, V., Talvala, E., Antunez, E., Barth, A., Adams, A., Horowitz, M., Levoy, M.: High performance imaging using large camera arrays. ACM TOG 24(3), 765–776 (2005)
103. Wuermlin, S., Lamboray, E., Staadt, O.G., Gross, M.H.: 3d video recorder. In: Proc. of Pacific Graphics 2002, pp. 325–334 (2002)
104. Xu, W., Zhou, K., Yu, Y., Tan, Q., Peng, Q., Guo, B.: Gradient domain editing of deforming mesh sequences. ACM TOG 26(3), 84 (2007)
105. Xu, X., Li, B.: Learning motion correlation for tracking articulated human body with a rao-blackwellised particle filter. In: Proc. ICCV (2007)
106. Yonemoto, S., Arita, D., Taniguchi, R.: Real-time human motion analysis and ik-based human figure control. In: Proc. of IEEE Workshop on Human Motion, pp. 149–154 (2000)
107. Zitnick, C.L., Kang, S.B., Uyttendaele, M., Winder, S., Szeliski, R.: High-quality video view interpolation using a layered representation. ACM TOG 23(3), 600–608 (2004)

Chapter 9
Video-Based Tracking of Scanned Humans

In this chapter, we propose our first performance capture algorithm.
By combining an image-based 3D correspondence estimation al-
gorithm and a Guided Laplacian-based mesh deformation scheme
(Sect. 3.2.2), our system captures the performance of a moving sub-
ject from multiple video streams, while preserving the connectivity of
the underlying mesh structure over time.

Nowadays, reconstructing time-varying models of real-world human actors from multi-view video is still challenging. As presented in Sect. 8.1, optical marker-based motion capture systems are inappropriate for applications where interference with the scene is not allowed, such as 3D Video. Moreover, since most marker-less motion capture methods proposed so far are based on a kinematic skeleton structure, capturing people wearing anything more general then skin-tight clothing is difficult.

In contrast, in this chapter, we propose a flexible performance capture algorithm to reconstruct the motion and the deforming geometry of a recorded subject, even when he/she is wearing arbitrary clothing, including a wide t-shirt, a skirt, and a kimono. In addition, our algorithm delivers a triangle mesh representation that maintains its connectivity over time. Our method employs a high-quality laser-scan of the tracked subject as underlying scene representation, and uses an optical flow-based 3D correspondence estimation method to guide the deformations of the model over time, such that it follows the motion of the actor in the input multi-view video streams.

The main contribution of this chapter is

- a complete framework to accurately and automatically track the motion and the time-varying non-rigid surface deformation of people wearing everyday apparel from a handful of multi-view video streams [1].

The remainder of this chapter is structured as follows: Sect. 9.1 describes the details of our performance capture technique. Afterwards, experiments and results with both synthetic and captured real-world data are presented in Sect. 9.2.

E. de Aguiar: Animation & Performance Capture Using Digi. Models, COSMOS 5, pp. 75–86.
springerlink.com   © Springer-Verlag Berlin Heidelberg 2010

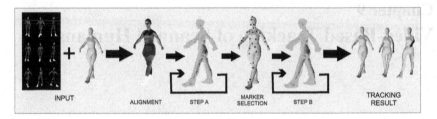

Fig. 9.1 Overview of our first performance capture framework. Given a laser-scan of a person and a multi-view video sequence showing her motion, the method deforms the scan in the same way as its real-world counterpart in the video streams. Reprinted from [1] © 2007 IEEE.

9.1 Framework

An overview of our performance capture technique is shown in Fig. 9.1. The input comprises of a static laser-scanned triangle mesh $\mathcal{M}_{tri}$ of the moving subject, and a multi-view video (MVV) sequence that shows the person moving arbitrarily. After data acquisition, we first align the laser scan to the pose of the person in the first time step of video, Sect. 9.1.1. Our framework comprises of two different tracking procedures, step A and step B, that are subsequently applied. In step A, we apply an iterative 3D flow-based deformation scheme to extract the motion information of each vertex over time from the images, Sect. 9.1.2. The results of step A quickly deteriorate due to accumulation of correspondence estimation errors. Nonetheless, they give us the possibility to automatically identify N marker vertices that can be tracked reliably, Sect. 9.1.3. Tracking step B, Sect. 9.1.4, is more robust against flow errors since it implicitly enforces structural integrity of the underlying mesh. It uses the moving marker vertices as deformation constraints to drive a Laplacian-based deformation scheme that makes all vertices correctly follow the motion of the actor in all video frames.

9.1.1 Acquisition and Initial Alignment

For each subject, we acquire the model and several multi-view video sequences in our studio, Chapter 4. After capturing the triangle mesh $\mathcal{M}_{tri}$, the subject immediately moves to the nearby area where he/she is recorded with our synchronized video cameras. After acquiring the sequence, silhouette images are calculated via color-based background subtraction, Sect. 2.3.1.

In an initial alignment, we register the scanned mesh with the pose of the person in the first time step of video. To this end, he/she initially strikes the same pose that he/she was scanned in. By means of an ICP-like registration the mesh is first coarsely aligned to a shape-from-silhouette reconstruction of the person. Thereafter, we run our flow-based Laplacian deformation scheme (Sect. 3.2.2) to correct for subtle non-rigid pose differences.

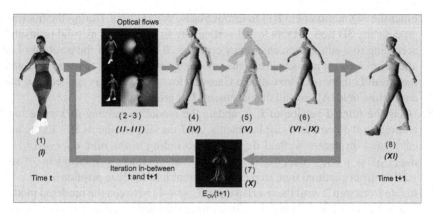

Fig. 9.2 The workflows of tracking steps A and B are very similar: Arabic numerals indicate the workflow specific to step A as it is described in Sect. 9.1.2, whereas Roman numerals denote step B which is detailed in Sect. 9.1.4. Reprinted from [1] © 2007 IEEE.

9.1.2 Step A: Purely Flow-Driven Tracking

After initial alignment, we iteratively deform each individual vertex of the mesh $\mathcal{M}_{tri}$ based on 3D flow fields that have been reconstructed from the multi-view images. As none structural information about the underlying shape of the model is considered, each vertex moves individually without considering the motion of its neighbors. This makes this simple procedure not robust against errors in the 3D flow field and leads to accumulation of correspondence estimation errors over time. However, this simple step still allows us to deduce valuable motion information about certain vertices on the surface which we can capitalize on in step B, where structural information about the underlying model is used to improve the tracking. Using subsequent time steps t and $t + 1$, our purely flow-driven tracking approach consists of the following steps (see Fig. 9.2):

1. Projectively texture the model using the images $I_t^0 \cdots I_t^{K-1}$ recorded with the K cameras at time step t and blend them according to the weights described in Sect. 12.1. From now on, for all deformation iterations between t and $t + 1$, the texture coordinates are fixed.
2. Generate K temporary images $T_t^0 \cdots T_t^{K-1}$ by projecting the textured model back into all K camera views.
3. Calculate K 2D optical flow fields $\mathbf{o}^k(T_t^k, I_{t+1}^k)$ between image T_t^k and I_{t+1}^k with $k = \{0 \cdots K - 1\}$.
4. Given the model, calibrated cameras, and the optical flow fields for all camera views, we can compute the 3D motion field, also known as the scene flow, by solving a linear system for each vertex v_i that is visible from at least two camera views, Sect. 2.3.3. The generated 3D flow field $\mathbf{f}(v_i) = (x_i, y_i, z_i)$ is parameterized over the mesh's surface, and it describes the displacement by which v_i should move from its current position.

5. Filter the 3D motion field $\mathbf{f}(\cdot)$ to remove noise and outliers. During the filtering process, the 3D flow vectors for all vertices are first classified as valid or invalid according to a silhouette-consistency criterion: $\mathbf{f}(\cdot)$ is valid if the position of v_i after displacement projects inside the silhouette images for all camera views and it is invalid otherwise. Thereafter, a Gaussian low-pass kernel is applied over the entire flow field. All invalid displacements $\mathbf{f}(\cdot)$ are set to zero.

6. Using the filtered version of $\mathbf{f}(\cdot)$, update the model by moving its vertices according to the computed displacements. Add the displacements $\mathbf{f}(\cdot)$ to the accumulated displacement field $\mathbf{d}_{\mathrm{ACCUM}}(\cdot)$ according to the rule: $\mathbf{d}_{\mathrm{ACCUM}}(v_i) = \mathbf{d}_{\mathrm{ACCUM}}(v_i) + \mathbf{f}(v_i)$. $\mathbf{d}_{\mathrm{ACCUM}}(\cdot)$ describes the complete displacement of all vertices from captured time step t to the current intermediate position.

7. Iterate from step 2 until the overlap error $E_{ov}(t+1)$ between the rendered model silhouettes (see Fig. 9.2) and the video-image silhouettes at time $t+1$ in all camera views is below $\mathrm{TR}_{\mathrm{OV}}$. $E_{ov}(t+1)$ is efficiently implemented on the GPU as a pixel-wise XOR [4].

8. Update the complete motion field $\mathbf{d}(t,v_i)$, which describes the displacement of each vertex v_i from time step 0 to t, according to $\mathbf{d}(t,v_i) = \mathbf{d}(t-1,v_i) + \mathbf{d}_{\mathrm{ACCUM}}(v_i)$.

The mesh $\mathcal{M}_{tri}$ is tracked over the whole sequence by applying the previously described steps to all pairs of consequent time steps. As a result, a complete motion field $\mathbf{d}(t,v_i)$ is generated for each vertex v_i that describes its displacement over time.

Since our scheme calculates $3D$ displacements without taking into account a priori information about the shape of the model, deformation errors accumulate over time. Step B solves this problem by explicitly enforcing structural properties of $\mathcal{M}_{tri}$ during tracking. To this end, the model is deformed based on constraints derived from reliably tracked marker vertices. These vertices are automatically selected from the results of step A based on the method described in the following section.

9.1.3 Automatic Marker Selection

Based on the deformation results of step A, our approach selects N marker vertices of the model that were accurately tracked over time. To this end, we first choose L candidate vertices for markers that are regularly distributed over the model's surface, Fig. 9.3(a). To find these candidates, we segment the surface of the mesh by means of a curvature-based segmentation approach [8]. This algorithm creates surface patches with similar numbers of vertices whose boundaries do not cross important shape features. In each region, the vertex located nearest to the center of gravity is selected as a candidate.

A candidate v_i is considered a marker vertex if it has a low error according to the two spatio-temporal selection criteria $tsc(\cdot)$ and $mov(\cdot)$. $tsc(\cdot)$ penalizes marker candidates that do not project into the silhouettes in all camera views and at all time steps. $mov(\cdot)$ penalizes candidates whose motions are not consistent with the

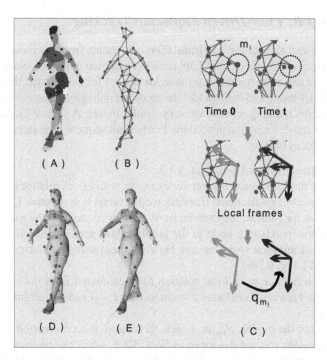

Fig. 9.3 (a) Segmented mesh $\mathcal{M}_{tri}$ and marker candidates (Sect. 9.1.3); **(b)** Graph connecting marker vertices; **(c)** Rotation for each m_i calculated according to the change in its local frame from time 0 to t; **(d-e)** Model is reconstructed subject to constraints derived from the motion of the markers. Reprinted from [1] © 2007 IEEE.

average motion of all vertices in the model. This way, we can prevent the placement of constraints in surface areas for which the flow estimates might be inaccurate. The two functions are defined as follows:

$$tsc(v_i) = \frac{1}{N_F * K} \sum_{t=0}^{N_F} \sum_{k=0}^{K} (1 - PROJ_{sil}^k(p_i + \mathbf{d}(t, v_i), t)) \tag{9.1}$$

$$mov(v_i) = \frac{1}{N_F} \sum_{t=0}^{N_F} (\|\mathbf{d}(t, v_i) - \frac{1}{N_V} \sum_{j=0}^{N_V} \mathbf{d}(t, v_j)\|) \tag{9.2}$$

N_F is the number of frames in the sequence, N_V is the number of vertices in the model, and p_i is the position of v_i at the first time step. $PROJ_{sil}^k(x, t)$ is a function that evaluates to 1 if a 3D point x projects inside the silhouette image of camera view k at time step t, and it is 0 otherwise. A candidate v_i is accepted as a marker vertex if $tsc(v_i) < \text{TR}_{\text{TSC}}$ and $mov(v_i) < \text{TR}_{\text{MOV}}$. Appropriate thresholds TR_{TSC} and TR_{MOV} are found through experiments. The index i of each marker v_i is then stored in the set $\mathcal{Q}$.

9.1.4   Step B: Flow-Driven Laplacian Tracking

In step B, we extract rotation and translation constraints from the motion of the N marker vertices to drive a Guided Laplacian deformation approach, Sect. 3.2.2. By this means we can extract novel motion fields $\mathbf{d}(t, v_i)$ for each vertex that make the model correctly move and deform like the recorded individual. The individual steps of the Laplacian tracking scheme are very similar to step A (Fig. 9.2), but differ in the details of the deformation procedure. For two subsequent time steps t and $t + 1$, tracking works as follows:

I-V   are identical to steps 1-5 in Sect. 9.1.2.

VI   From the motion of each marker vertex $m_i{=}v_i$, with $i \in \mathcal{Q}$, relative to the default position, a set of rotation and translation constraints is computed. Local coordinate frames for each m_i are derived from a graph connecting the markers. Each marker corresponds to a node in the graph. Edges are constructed by building an extended minimal spanning tree between them using geodesics as distance measure [5], Fig. 9.3(b).

VII   For each marker m_i, a local rotation R_i is estimated from the change of its local frame between its reference orientation at $t = 0$ and its current orientation, Fig. 9.3(c).

VIII   Thereafter, the model $\mathcal{M}'_{tri}$ in its new target pose is reconstructed by applying the deformation method described in Sect. 3.2.2, subject to position constraints pc, derived from the position of the markers m, and the calculated rotation constraints $R = q \cdot m_i$, Fig. 9.3(d-e).

IX   Update the accumulated displacement field for all vertices $\mathbf{d}_{\mathrm{ACCUM}}(\cdot)$ according to the rule: $\mathbf{d}_{\mathrm{ACCUM}}(v_i) = p_i^{REC} - p_i - \mathbf{d}(t-1, m_i)$, where p_i^{REC} is the reconstructed vertex position for v_i.

X   Iterate from step II until the overlap error $E_{ov}(t+1)$ between rendered model silhouettes and video-image silhouettes in all cameras at $t + 1$ is below a threshold $\mathrm{TR}_{\mathrm{OV}}$.

XI   Update the complete motion field $\mathbf{d}(t, v_i)$ by $\mathbf{d}(t, v_i) = \mathbf{d}(t-1, v_i) + \mathbf{d}_{\mathrm{ACCUM}}(v_i)$.

By applying this algorithm to all subsequent time steps we can track the model $\mathcal{M}_{tri}$ over the whole video sequence. The Laplacian scheme reconstructs the mesh in its new pose in a way that it preserves the differential surface properties of the original scan. Due to this implicit shape regularization, our tracking approach in step B is robust against inaccurate flow estimates and deforms the mesh in accordance to its real-world counterpart in the video streams. Thanks to the guided Laplacian-based scheme, details and features of the mesh are preserved. The resulting scanned model is correctly reconstructed at all frames of the input video sequence and rigid and non-rigid surface deformations are captured, Sect. 9.2.

9.2   Results and Discussion

Our framework has been tested on several synthetic and captured real-world data sets. Synthetic sequences enable us to compare our results against the ground truth.

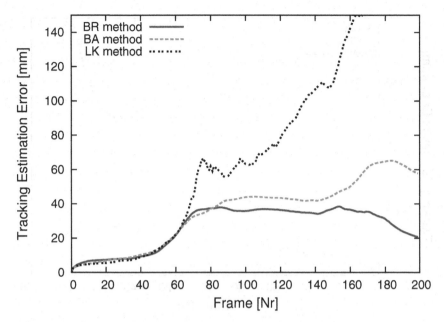

Fig. 9.4 Three different optical flow methods have been tested with our framework. The average vertex position errors for each frame relative to the ground truth are plotted in this figure. The method by Brox et al. (Sect. 2.3.2) (red line) shows the best performance. Reprinted from [1] © 2007 IEEE.

They were generated by animating a textured scan of a woman ($26K\triangle$) provided by Cyberware™ (Fig. 9.1) with publicly available motion capture files showing soccer moves and a simple walk. Output streams were rendered into eight virtual cameras (1004x1004 pixels, 25 fps) that were placed in a circular arrangement like in our real studio, Chapter 4. Gaussian noise was purposefully added to the images to mimic the characteristics of our real cameras. We ran a series of experiments to evaluate the performance of different algorithmic alternatives and to decide on the best optical flow estimation scheme for our purpose.

The latter question was answered by our first experiment. To test a representative set of alternative flow algorithms, we compared the results obtained by using our complete tracking framework (steps A and B) in conjunction with the local Lukas Kanade method [6] (*LK*), the dense optical flow method by Black et al. [2] (*BA*), and the warping-based method for dense optical flow by Brox et al. [3] (*BR*), Sect. 2.3.2. The plot in Fig. 9.4 shows the average position errors between ground truth and tracking results for each frame of a walking sequence. By using the local Lukas Kanade method, we are unable to track the mesh and the error constantly increases over time. The error plot for *BA* is much better, but it is clearly outperformed by *BR*. The positional inaccuracy obtained with *BR* never exceeds 4 cm and even decreases after a peak in the middle. Note that the synthetic model (Fig. 9.1) is textured with very uniform colors which makes optical flow computation extremely hard. Even on

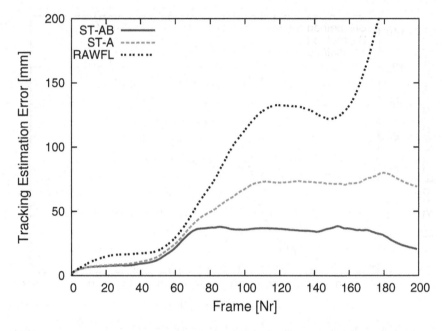

Fig. 9.5 Average tracking error for all time steps of the synthetic walking sequence obtained with different mesh tracking alternatives. The pipeline we propose (ST-AB) clearly produces the best results. Reprinted from [1] © 2007 IEEE.

such difficult data, *BR* tracks the mesh reliably, and thus the method by Brox et al. is our method of choice for flow estimation.

In a second experiment, we compared the different deformation alternatives, namely deformation along the unfiltered flow (*RAWFL*), deformation according to step A only (*ST-A*), and deformation with our complete pipeline (*ST-AB*). Fig. 9.5 plots the average vertex position error against the frame number. Using *RAWFL*, the measurement error grows almost exponentially. Tracking with a filtered flow field leads to significantly better results, but the absolute inaccuracy is still comparably high. In contrast, our complete pipeline leads to a very low peak position error of 3.5 cm that even decreases over time.

Table 9.1 summarizes the results that we obtained by assessing different combinations of mesh tracking and flow computation methods. The column *TIME* contains the time needed on a Pentium IV with 3GHz to compute the deformation from one video time step t to the next one $t + 1$. We also analyzed the average volume change over the whole sequence, *VOLCHG*, in order to get a numerical indicator for unreasonable deformations. The preservation of mesh quality is analyzed by looking at the average distortion of the triangles, *MQLT*. It is computed by averaging the per-triangle Frobenius norm over the mesh and over time [7]. This norm is 0 for an equilateral triangle and approaches infinity with increasing degeneracy. Finally, the

Table 9.1 Different algorithmic alternatives are compared in terms of run time, volume change (*VOLCHG*), mesh quality (*MQLT*), and position error (*ERROR*). Our proposed pipeline with the dense optical flow method by Brox et al. (*ST-AB/BR*) leads to the best results. Reprinted from [1] © 2007 IEEE.

METHOD	TIME	VOLCHG	MQLT	ERROR
RAWFL	109s	17.65%	0.46	98.66mm
ST-A	111s	4.97%	0.30	49.39mm
BR / ST-AB	111s	2.79%	0.035	26.45mm
BA	426s	2.77%	0.029	35.28mm
LK	89s	10.73%	1.72	76.24mm

column labeled *ERROR* contains the average of the position error over all vertices and time steps.

The run times of the first three alternatives are almost identical since 109 s have to be spent on the calculation of the eight megapixel optical flow fields. Even in our complete pipeline, the deformation itself runs at almost interactive frame rates since the involved linear systems can be solved quickly. As expected, the tracking error is highest if one deforms $\mathcal{M}_{tri}$ using the unfiltered flow, *RAWFL*. Furthermore, the mesh distortion is fairly high and the volume change rises to implausible values. The best overall performance is achieved when we use our complete pipeline *ST-AB/BR*. Here, the position error is lowest, the volume change is in the range of normal non-rigid body deformations, and the triangles remain in nice shape. Although the alternative *BA* produces a fairly low triangle distortion, its run time is four times slower than the best alternative and the resulting positional accuracy is almost 1 cm lower. *LK* is fastest, but leads to bad results according to all other criteria. Our tests thus confirm that the complete tracking pipeline in combination with a high-quality dense flow method can reliably track human motion from raw unmodified video streams.

For our tests with real data we captured video footage and body models for different male and female test subjects using the setup described in Chapter. 4. The captured video sequences are between 300 and 600 frames long and show a variety of different clothing styles, including normal everyday apparel and a traditional Japanese kimono. Many different motions have been captured ranging from simple walking to gymnastic moves.

Fig. 9.6 shows several side-by-side comparisons between input video frames and recovered mesh poses. The algorithm reliably recovers the pose and surface deformation for the male subject who wears comparably wide apparel. This is also confirmed by the very precise overlap between the reprojected model and the input image silhouettes. Our algorithm can even capture the motion and the cloth deformation for a woman wearing a kimono, Fig. 9.6 and Fig. 9.7. Since the limbs are completely occluded, this would not have been possible with a normal motion capture approach.

The results show that our purely passive performance capture approach can automatically capture both pose and surface deformation of human actors. It illustrates

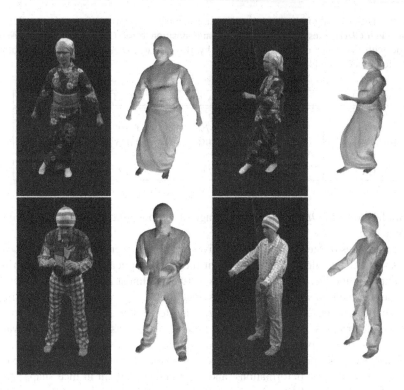

Fig. 9.6 Side-by-side comparisons between an input video frame and the pose of the laser scan that our approach reconstructed. The poses of the persons and even the deformations of complex apparel, like the kimono, are faithfully reproduced. Reprinted from [1] © 2007 IEEE.

that a skeleton-less algorithm is capable of tracking even complex deformations of different materials by means of the same framework. Our system neither requires any segmentation of the model into parts, e.g. clothing and body, nor does it expect the specification of explicit material parameters as they are often used in garment motion tracking. Both of this would be very difficult for a human wearing different kinds of fabrics. The combination of an a priori model, a fast Laplacian deformation scheme, and a 3D flow-based correspondence estimation method enables us to capture complex shape deformations from only a few cameras. As an additional benefit, our method preserves the mesh's connectivity which is particularly important for model-based 3D Video applications, Chapter 12.

Nonetheless, our algorithm is subject to a few limitations. Currently, our Guided Laplacian-based scheme cannot handle volume constraints. In some situations such a constraint may prevent incorrect mesh deformations and thus compensate the effect of incorrect flow estimates. However, for some types of apparel, such as a long skirt or our kimono, a volume constraint may even prevent correct tracking. From this point of view our system is more flexible. Another limitation arises if the

Fig. 9.7 Our method realistically captures the motion and the dynamic shape of a woman wearing a Japanese kimono from only eight video streams. Reprinted from [1] © 2007 IEEE.

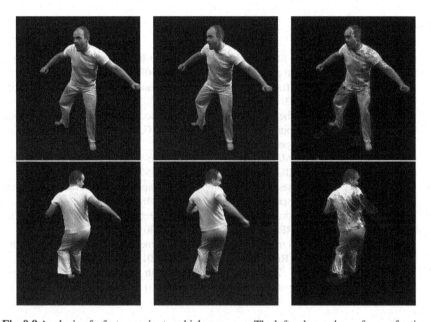

Fig. 9.8 Analysis of a fast capoeira turn kick sequence. The left column shows frames for time t, the middle column shows frames for time $t + 1$, and the right column shows the frames from t morphed onto time $t + 1$ using the dense optical flow method by Brox et al. **Top row**: For motion at normal speed, the flow field produces good results, and therefore the extracted 3D deformation constraints enables our framework to correctly track the motion of the subject. **Bottom row**: If the motion is very fast, however, the optical flow is not able to compute reliable correspondences anymore, as seen by the erroneous warp.

subject in the scene moves very quickly, since in these situations optical flow tracking may fail, Fig. 9.8. One way to attack this problem is to use a high-speed camera for capturing fast scenes. However, they are more expensive and would require more computation power. Another option is to combine our Laplacian-tracking scheme with a marker-less 3D feature tracking algorithm that jointly uses image features and optical flow to handle faster scenes, Chapter 10.

Finally, our algorithm cannot capture the true shape variation of low-frequency surface details, such as wrinkles in clothing. While they globally deform with the model, they seem to be "baked in" to the surface. In Chapter 11, we show that more fine details can be captured by employing a silhouette rim-based method and a multi-view stereo algorithm.

Despite these limitations, our method is a flexible and reliable purely passive method to capture the motion and time-varying shape of moving subjects from a handful of video streams. Our algorithm can handle a large range of human motions and clothing styles, making a laser scan of a subject move and deform in the same way as its real-world counterpart in video.

References

1. de Aguiar, E., Theobalt, C., Stoll, C., Seidel, H.P.: Marker-less deformable mesh tracking for human shape and motion capture. In: Proc. CVPR (2007)
2. Black, M., Anandan, P.: A framework for the robust estimation of optical flow. In: Proc. of ICCV, pp. 231–236 (1993)
3. Brox, T., Bruhn, A., Papenberg, N., Weickert, J.: High accuracy optical flow estimation based on a theory for warping. In: Pajdla, T., Matas, J(G.) (eds.) ECCV 2004. LNCS, vol. 3024, pp. 25–36. Springer, Heidelberg (2004)
4. Carranza, J., Theobalt, C., Magnor, M., Seidel, H.P.: Free-viewpoint video of human actors. ACM TOG (Proc. of SIGGRAPH 2003) 22(3), 569–577 (2003)
5. Kruskal, J.B.: On the shortest spanning subtree of a graph and the traveling salesman problem. Proc. of the American Mathematical Society 7, 48–50 (1956)
6. Lucas, B., Kanade, T.: An iterative image registration technique with an application to stereo vision. In: Proc. DARPA IU Workshop, pp. 121–130 (1981)
7. Pebay, P.P., Baker, T.J.: A comparison of triangle quality measures. In: Proceedings to the 10th International Meshing Roundtable, pp. 327–340 (2001)
8. Yamauchi, H., Gumhold, S., Zayer, R., Seidel, H.P.: Mesh segmentation driven by gaussian curvature. Visual Computer 21(8-10), 649–658 (2005)

Chapter 10
Feature Tracking for Mesh-Based Performance Capture

In this chapter, we propose our second performance capture frame-work. First, a robust method to track 3D trajectories of features on a moving subject recorded with multiple cameras is described. Thereafter, by combining the 3D trajectories with a mesh deformation scheme, the performance of a moving actor is captured and the high-quality scanned model can be directly animated such that it mimics the subject's motion.

As described in Chapter 8, the generation of realistic and lifelike animated characters from captured real-world motion sequences is still a hard and time-consuming task. In the previous chapter, we presented our first performance capture system, that uses an optical flow-based 3D correspondence estimation method to capture the motion and dynamic shape of the moving actor. Although achieving good results, as mentioned in Sect. 9.2, one of the main limitations of the previous approach is its lack of robustness when the motion sequence is fast or complex.

In this chapter, we present an alternative solution, that improves the performance of the previous technique, by combining a flow-based and an image-feature based method. Furthermore, we divide the problem into two steps: first, image features in 3D space are robustly identified and tracked. Afterwards, using the 3D trajectories of the features as constraints in a Laplacian-based tracking scheme, Sect. 3.2.2, the scanned model is realistically animated over time. The simple and robust algorithm proposed here creates shape deformations for the scanned model without specification of explicit material parameters, and it works even for arbitrary moving subjects or people wearing wide and loose apparel.

The main contributions of this chapter is

- a simple and robust method to automatically identify important features and track their 3D trajectories on arbitrary subjects from multi-view video [1],
- and an efficient Laplacian-based tracking scheme that uses only a handful of feature trajectories to realistically animate a scanned model of the recorded subject [1].

E. de Aguiar: Animation & Performance Capture Using Digi. Models, COSMOS 5, pp. 87–99.
springerlink.com

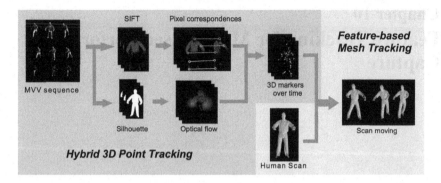

Fig. 10.1 Overview of our second performance capture framework: given a multi-view video sequence showing a moving subject, our method automatically identifies features and tracks their 3D trajectories. By applying the captured trajectories to a static laser-scan of the subject, we are able to realistically animate the scanned model making it move the same way as its real-world counterpart in the video streams.

The remainder of this chapter is structured as follows: Sect. 10.1 briefly describes our second performance capture framework. Thereafter, Sect. 10.2 details the automatic approach to identify features and track their 3D trajectories over time. Sect. 10.3 describes the Laplacian-based tracking scheme used to animate the scanned model according to the constraints derived from the estimated 3D point trajectories. Results with several captured real-world sequences and discussion are presented in Sect. 10.4.

10.1   Overview

An overview of our second performance capture approach is shown in Fig. 10.1. Our system expects a multi-view video (MVV) sequence as input that shows the subject moving arbitrarily. After acquiring the sequence in our studio, Chapter 4, silhouette images are calculated via color-based background subtraction (Sect. 2.3.1), and we use the synchronized video streams to extract and track important features in 3D space over time, Sect. 10.2.

Our hybrid 3D point tracking framework jointly uses two techniques to estimate the 3D trajectories of the features from unmodified multi-view video streams. First, features in the images are identified using the Scale Invariant Feature Transform (SIFT), Sect. 2.3.4. Furthermore, SIFT is able to match a feature to its corresponding one from a different camera viewpoint. This allows us to generate a set of pairwise pixel correspondences between different camera views for each time step of input video. Unfortunately, tracking the features over time using only local descriptors is not robust if the human subject is wearing sparsely textured clothing. Therefore, we use a robust dense optical flow method as an additional step to track the features for each camera view separately in order to fill the gaps in the SIFT tracking. By merging both sources of information, we are able to reconstruct the 3D trajectories for many features over the whole sequence.

Our hybrid technique is able to correctly identify and track many 3D points. In addition to the estimation of 3D point positions, our approach also calculates a confidence value for each estimation, which indicates how reliable a particular feature has been located. Using confidence-weighted feature trajectories as deformation constraints in the guided Laplacian-based method described in Sect. 3.2.2, our system robustly brings a static laser-scanned mesh $\mathcal{M}_{tri}$ of the subject into life, by making it follow the motion of the recorded actor.

10.2 Hybrid 3D Point Tracking

Our hybrid framework jointly employs local descriptors and dense optical flow to identify features and estimate their 3D positions over time from multiple calibrated camera views. In contrast to many other approaches [2, 4, 5], we developed an automatic tracking algorithm that works directly on the images and does not require any a priori knowledge about the moving subject. It is our goal to create a simple and generic algorithm that can be used to track features on rigid bodies, articulated objects, and non-rigidly deforming subjects in the same way. Therefore, at this point, we do not use shape information about the subject.

The input to our algorithm is comprised of synchronized video streams recorded by K cameras, each containing N video frames, Fig. 10.2(a). In the first step, we automatically identify L important features, also called keypoints, for each camera view k and time step t, and generate a set of local descriptors $F_{k,t} = \{f_{k,t}^0, \dots, f_{k,t}^L\}$ using SIFT [6] (see also Sect. 2.3.4).

Since the SIFT descriptors are robust against image scale, rotation, change in viewpoints, and change in illumination, they can be used to find corresponding features across different camera views. Given an image $I_{k,t}$, from camera view k and time step t, and the respective set of SIFT descriptors $F_{k,t}$, we try to match each element of $F_{k,t}$ with the set of keypoints from all other camera views. We use a matching function similar to [6], which assigns a match between $f_{k,t}^i$ and a keypoint in $F_{j,t}$ if the Euclidean distance between their invariant descriptor vectors is minimum. In order to discard false correspondences, nearest neighbor distance ratio matching is used with a threshold T_{MATCH} [7].

After matching the keypoints across all K camera views at individual time steps, we gather all R correct pairwise matches into a list of pixel correspondences $C_t = \{c_t^0, \dots, c_t^R\}$, by using all reliable matches found for each time step t, Fig. 10.2(c). Each element $c_t^r = ((cam_u, P_t^i), (cam_v, P_t^j))$ stores the information about a correspondence between two different camera views, i.e. that pixel P_t^i in camera cam_u corresponds to pixel P_t^j in camera view cam_v at time t.

Unfortunately, tracking the features over time using only the list of correspondences C and connecting their elements at different time steps is not robust, because it is very unlikely that the same feature will be found at all time instants. This is specially true if the captured images show subjects performing fast movements, where

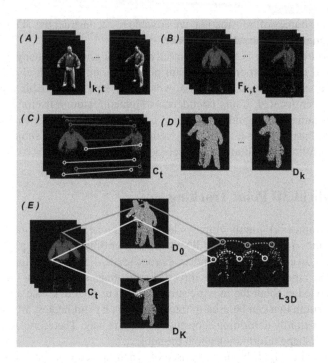

Fig. 10.2 Using the synchronized video streams as input (**a**), our hybrid approach first identifies features in the images using SIFT (**b**), and then matches these features between different pairs of camera views based on their descriptors (**c**). In addition, we track these features for each camera view separately using optical flow (**d**). At the end, reliable 3D trajectories for the features are reconstructed by merging both information (**e**).

features can be occluded for a long period of time, or when the subject wears everyday apparel with sparse texture. In the latter case, SIFT only detects a small number of keypoints per time step, which is usually not enough for tracking articulated objects. Therefore, in order to robustly reconstruct the 3D trajectories for the features, we decided to use optical flow to track both elements of all c_t^r for each camera view separately, i.e. the pixel P_t^i is tracked using camera view cam_u and the pixel P_t^j using camera view cam_v.

The 2D flow-based tracking method works as follows: for each camera view k, we track all pixels over time using the warping-based method for dense optical flow proposed by Brox et al. [3]. After calculating the optical flow $\mathbf{o}_k^t(I_{k,t}, I_{k,t+1})$ between time step t and $t+1$ for camera k, we use $\mathbf{o}_k^t$ to warp the image $I_{k,t}$ and we verify for each pixel in the warped image if it matches the corresponding pixel in $I_{k,t+1}$. We eliminate the pixels that do not have a partner in $t+1$, and the pixels that belong to the background by comparing the warped pixels with the pre-computed silhouette $SIL_{k,t+1}$. This process is repeated for all consecutive time steps and for all camera views. As a result, we construct a tracking list $D_k = \{E^0, \ldots, E^g\}$ with G pixel trajectories for each camera view k, Fig. 10.2(d). Each element $E^i = \{P_0^i, \ldots, P_N^i\}$ contains the positions of the pixel P_t^i for all time steps t.

The last step of our hybrid tracking scheme merges the optical flow tracking information with the list of correspondences to reconstruct the 3D trajectories for all features. We take pixel correspondences from all time steps into account. For instance, if a matching c_t^r is detected by SIFT only at the end of the sequence, we are still able to recover the anterior positions of the feature by using the optical flow information.

For each entry $c_t^r = ((cam_u, P_t^i), (cam_v, P_t^j))$, we verify if the pixel P_t^i is found in D_{cam_u} and if the pixel P_t^j is found in D_{cam_v}. In case both elements are found, we estimate the position of the respective 3D point, $mm_r(t)$, for the whole sequence, as shown in Fig. 10.2(e), otherwise c_t^r is discarded. The 3D positions are estimated by triangulating the viewing rays that start at the camera views cam_u and cam_v and pass through the respective image plane pixel at P_t^i and P_t^j. However, due to inaccuracies, these rays will not intersect exactly at a single point. In this case, we compute a pseudo-intersection point $pos_t^r = \{x, y, z\}$ that minimizes the sum of squared distance to each pointing ray. We also use the inverse of this distance, s_r, as a confidence measure indicating how reliable a particular feature has been located. If s_r is below a threshold T_{CONF} we discard it, since it indicates that c_t^r assigns a wrong pixel correspondence between two different camera views.

We also discard a trajectory mm_r if it does not project into the silhouettes in all camera views and at all time steps. This way, we can prevent the use of 3D points whose trajectories degenerate over time as deformation constraints. We assess silhouette-consistency using the following measure:

$$TSIL(mm_r) = \sum_{t=0}^{N} \sum_{k=0}^{K} PROJ_{sil}^k(pos_t^r, t), \quad (10.1)$$

where $PROJ_{sil}^k(pos_t^r, t)$ is a function that evaluates to 1 if $mm_r(t)$ projects inside the silhouette image of camera view k at time step t, and it is 0 otherwise. We only consider mm_r a reliable 3D trajectory if $TSIL(mm_r) > TR_{SIL}$. Appropriate values for the thresholds are found through experiments.

After processing all elements of C for all time steps, we generate a list with reliable 3D trajectories for the features. The list $L_{3D} = \{mm_0, \ldots, mm_h\} = \{(LP_0, LE_0), \ldots, (LP_H, LE_H)\}$ assigns to each trajectory mm_i, a tuple (LP_i, LE_i) containing the 3D point positions, $LP_i = \{pos_0^i, \ldots, pos_N^i\}$, and the respective list of confidence values for each estimated 3D position, $LE_i = \{s_0^i, \ldots, s_N^i\}$. As shown in Sect. 10.4, our hybrid approach is able to identify and accurately track many 3D points for sequences where the human subject is performing reasonably fast motion, even when he/she is dressed in everyday apparel.

10.3 Feature-Based Laplacian Mesh Tracking

Using the reconstructed 3D point trajectories, the performance of the moving subject can be captured using a scanned model of the real-world actor. For this purpose, we

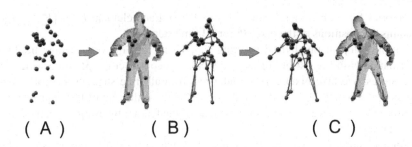

(A)   (B)   (C)

Fig. 10.3 After aligning the 3D point positions (**a**) with the scanned model at the reference time step (**b**), our method reconstructs a novel pose for $\mathcal{M}_{tri}$ by jointly using rotational and positional constraints on the marked vertices, derived from the 3D feature trajectories (**c**).

first roughly align the scan $\mathcal{M}_{tri}$ with the 3D point positions at the first time step of video (our reference), Fig. 10.3(a). This is automatically done by applying a PCA-based alignment scheme to a reconstructed volumetric shape-from-silhouette model of the moving subject. Afterwards, we select H marked vertices $V_T = \{v_{Th} | h \in \{0 \cdots H\}\}$ in $\mathcal{M}_{tri}$ by choosing vertices that are closest to the 3D point positions at the reference time step, Fig. 10.3(b). These marked vertices V_T are used to guide the Laplacian-based deformation technique (Sect. 3.2.2) that deforms the static scanned model over time mimicking its real-world counterpart in the input video.

In summary, the following procedure is performed for each time step t: first, we calculate the local rotations R that should be applied to the marked vertices of $\mathcal{M}_{tri}$. The local rotation for each marked vertex v_{Th} is calculated from the rotation of the corresponding 3D point $mm_h(t)$ between reference time and time t by means of a graph-based method, Sect. 9.1.4. Since we want the marked vertices V_T to perform the same rotations as the 3D points, we set $R_{v_{Th}} = R_{mm_h(t)}$ for all H 3D points. Thereafter, we apply the Laplacian-based deformation method described in Sect. 3.2.2 to reconstruct the vertex positions of $\mathcal{M}'_{tri}$, such that it best approximates the rotated differential coordinates R, as well as the positional constraints pc, with $pc = pos_t$ for all marked vertices at time t.

In Eq. 3.5, the matrix A is a diagonal matrix containing non-zero weights $A_{ij} = c * s_t^j$, c being a constant, only for constrained vertices v_j. We weight the marked vertex position pos_t^j for v_{Tj} at time t proportionally with respect to its corresponding confidence value, since small values for s_t^j indicate inaccuracies in the estimated 3D position. This weighting scheme leads to a better visual animation quality for the animated human scans, Sect.10.4.

After applying this procedure to the whole sequence, the Laplacian-based tracking scheme is able to animate the scanned model making it correctly follow the motion of the actor recorded in all video frames. As shown in Sect. 10.4, our approach preserves the details and features of the mesh, and is able to generate plausible and realistic surface deformations for subjects wearing even loose everyday apparel.

Table 10.1 For each captured real-world sequence, the number of identified features (FEAT) and the average confidence value (S) are shown. We also employ accuracy and quality measures for the animated scan, i.e. changes in volume (VOL), distortion of triangles (QLT), and multi-view silhouette overlap (OVL), to demonstrate the performance of our performance capture framework.

SEQ	FEAT	S $[m^{-1}]$	OVLP	VOL	QLT
CAPO	1207	65.18	95.4%	3.2%	0.03
DANC	1232	58.30	95.6%	1.8%	0.01
YOGA	1457	112.23	93.7%	3.6%	0.10
WALK	2920	71.78	95.5%	1.5%	0.01
DRSS	3132	45.72	94.4%	2.0%	0.01

10.4 Results and Discussion

We tested our framework on several real-world sequences with different male and female test subjects recorded in our studio, Chapter 4. Our acquisition procedure is similar to the one described in Sect. 9.2. The captured video sequences are between 150 and 400 frames long, and show a variety of different clothing styles and motions, ranging from simple walking to yoga and capoeira moves.

As shown in the second and third columns of Table 10.1, our hybrid 3D point tracking approach is able to identify and track many features in 3D space accurately. The average confidence value (S) for the 3D point positions are large, i.e. corresponding to position errors of around $1.0 - 2.2cm$, which indicates that correct correspondences between different camera views are found over the whole sequence. Three different frames for the yoga (YOGA) and walking (WALK) sequences, with selected features shown as dots, can be seen in the upper and middle rows of Fig. 10.4. Looking at the temporal evolution, one can see that the features are reliably tracked over time. The lower images of Fig. 10.4 also show three closeups of the legs in the walking sequence. Features were accurately tracked, despite the appearance ambiguities caused by the trousers with homogeneous color. If we had used only SIFT descriptors to track these features, it would have been impossible to track them in these homogeneous areas. In this case, the pixel correspondences would be removed due to T_{MATCH}, or the features would be matched in a wrong way, i.e. features from one side of the trousers would have been matched against the ones in the other side.

High tracking accuracy and reliability even in such difficult situations is upheld by additionally taking into account optical flow information. Even if a correspondence was only found for one time step, we can reconstruct the complete trajectory for this feature by looking at the optical flow information. This second source of information also enables us to apply a very high threshold T_{MATCH} which eliminates unreliable 3D feature matches already at an early stage. Using only the reliable ones, optical flow robustly tracks the features separately in each camera view, and at the end, we merge both results to reconstruct the 3D point trajectories.

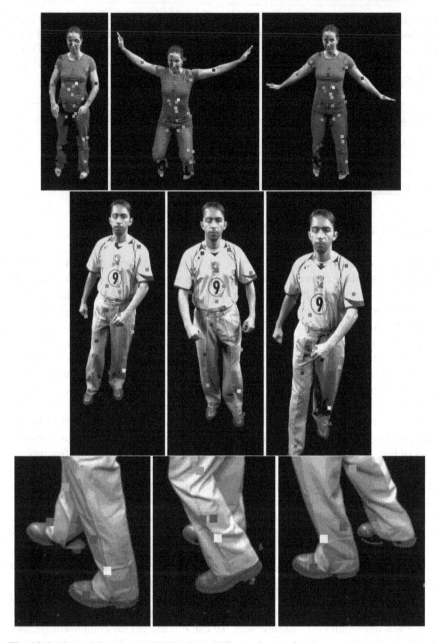

Fig. 10.4 Selected features tracked in three different frames for the yoga (**upper row**) and walking sequences (**middle row**) and three frames of the walking sequence in detail (**lower row**). Our hybrid framework correctly identifies and tracks 3D trajectories of features even in the presence of occlusions or appearance ambiguities.

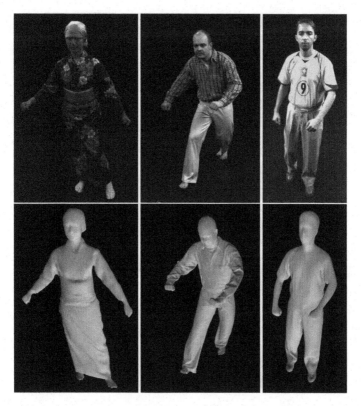

Fig. 10.5 Side-by-side comparisons between input video frames and reconstructed poses for the human scan. By combining the 3D point trajectories tracked with the Laplacian-based deformation scheme, our algorithm is able to directly animate a human body scan.

Before using the 3D point trajectories to guide the deformation of the scanned model $\mathcal{M}_{tri}$ we first choose a subset of N_M points from the initial set of 3D trajectories L_{3D} at the reference time step. This subset of points should be distributed evenly on the model surface. This is done by ramdonly choosing an element in L_{3D} and all adjacent points next to it at the reference time step by using a distance threshold T_{DIST}. We compare the confidence values for this group of elements and choose the point with the maximum confidence value. We continue the same procedure choosing another point in L_{3D} until all selected points are separated by a distance T_{DIST}, and consequently distributed over the model's surface. We conducted several experiments with different values for T_{DIST}, and found out that in general, values between $10cm$ and $20cm$ produce best results. For a typical sequence, this leads to around $20 - 50$ selected points. Note that although our hybrid 3D tracking approach is able to correctly track many more points over time, even a subset of points is sufficient to track body poses reliably. Our selection criteria also enable us to eliminate multiple trajectories of the same feature (stemming for different camera pairs), which bears no useful information.

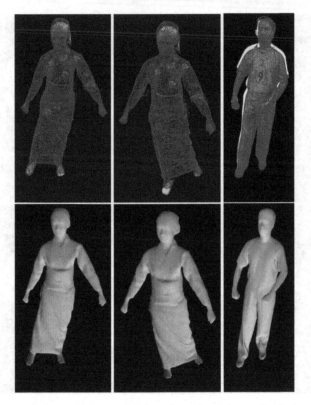

Fig. 10.6 Overlap between reprojected model (red) and input image for the female and male subjects. Our framework is able to correctly reconstruct their pose even when they are wearing wide and loose apparel.

Fig. 10.5 show several side-by-side comparisons between input video frames and tracked poses of the human scan. Our algorithm reliably recovers the poses and creates plausible and realistic surface deformations for the male actor performing a capoeira move, and even for the female subject wearing a long dress. Due to the occlusion of the limbs or the wide and loose apparel, tracking the motion of these subjects over time would have been hard with a normal motion capture system.

Due to the lack of ground truth for our experiments, we evaluate our results by overlapping the reprojected model with the input images as shown in Fig. 10.6. We also calculate a multi-view overlap measure by counting the average number of pixels that do not match between the reprojected model and the input image silhouettes for all camera views and all time steps. As shown in the plot in Fig. 10.7, our system automatically animates the human scan making it follow the motion of the real-world actor with a consistent silhouette-accuracy of more than 94%.

We also performed experiments to evaluate the performance of our framework in animating the human scan. Table 10.1 summarizes the results we have obtained employing quality and accuracy measures for several sequences. The column *VOL*

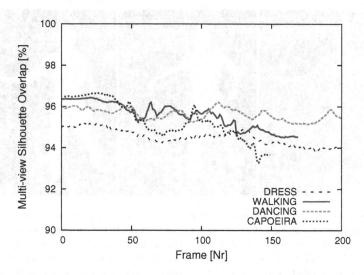

Fig. 10.7 Multi-view silhouette overlap for several captured sequences. Our system accurately makes the static human scan follow the motion of the captured real-world actor.

shows the average volume change in the animated scan over the whole sequence relative to the initial scanned model. This measure is a numerical indicator for implausible deformations. The preservation of mesh quality is analyzed by looking at the average distortion of the triangles, *QLT*. It is computed by averaging the per-triangle Frobenius norm over the mesh and over time [8]. This norm is 0 for an equilateral triangle and approaches infinity with increasing degeneracy. Finally, the column labeled *OVLP* contains the average multi-view overlap between the reprojected model and the input image silhouettes over time.

Table 10.1 shows that the volume change in the animated human scan is in the range of normal non-rigid body deformations, and that triangles remain in nice shape. It also shows that the Laplacian-based deformation approach reconstructs the poses of the scan with high accuracy, even if the subjects wear wide and loose everyday apparel.

We performed experiments to demonstrate the importance of the confidence value as a weight in Eq. 3.5 as well, Sect. 10.3. Our experiments show that when using the confidence value in the Laplacian-based scheme, surface deformations are generated in a more reasonable and lifelike way, which leads to a better visual reconstruction quality. On the other hand, when not using it, changes in volume and triangle distortions increase, which reduce the surface deformation quality and the multi-view silhouette-accuracy.

Our results show that our purely passive hybrid tracking method can automatically identify and track the 3D trajectories of features on a moving subject without the need of any a priori information or optical markers. By combining it with an efficient deformation technique, it also enables us to directly and realistically animate a static human scan making it follow the same motion as its real-world counterpart.

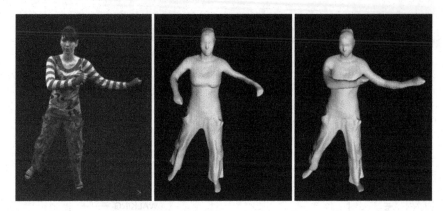

Fig. 10.8 Female jazz dance sequence: the left column shows the correct input pose, the middle column shows the slightly wrong pose captured if we apply the current performance capture method, and the right column shows the better result if we apply the improved method described in Chapter 11. While at some point in this complex sequence the feature trajectories at the hand and feet are lost with the current method, the analysis-through-synthesis framework, described in the next chapter, is able to accurately capture the female pose.

Nonetheless, our algorithm is subject to a few limitations. For the hybrid 3D point tracking approach, the time needed to identify and track the features per multi-view frame on a Pentium IV with 3GHz is around 3-5 minutes. Furthermore, it is hard to recover complete feature trajectories in scenes that show very rapid motion, complex occlusion situations, or many rotations that make across-camera correspondence finding difficult, see Fig. 10.8. A possible alternative to partly solve these limitations is to use a high-speed camera for capturing fast scenes. However, this may increase the run time of the system even further. For the feature-based Laplacian mesh tracking technique, although it correctly captures the body deformations at a coarse scale, depending on the number of tracked features used in the reconstruction process, the deformations of subtle details, such as small wrinkles, are not captured.

In Chapter 11, we present an improved performance capture framework that extends the capabilities of the current system, being able to reconstruct an unprecedented range of real-world scenes at a high level of detail. As shown in the side-by-side comparison in Fig. 10.8, the current method is not able to recover complete trajectories for some features in the hands and feet of the subject. As a result, it generates a slightly wrong pose for this complex sequence. In contrast, the analysis-through-synthesis framework presented in Chapter 11 faithfully reconstructs the pose. Furthermore, the proposed silhouette rim-based technique and the model-guided multi-view stereo approach are able to capture the dynamic subtle details more accurately.

Despite these limitations, the hybrid approach still has the advantage of being applicable in other problem settings where no geometry is available. Moreover, the current performance capture framework is able to move and deform a high-quality scanned model in the same way as its real-world counterpart, while preserving its connectivity over time. Our flexible algorithm does not require optical markings, and behaves robustly even for humans wearing sparsely textured and wide apparel.

References

1. de Aguiar, E., Theobalt, C., Stoll, C., Seidel, H.: Marker-less 3d feature tracking for mesh-based human motion capture. In: Proc. ICCV HUM 2007, pp. 1–15 (2007)
2. Balan, A., Black, M.: An adaptive appearance model approach for model-based articulated object tracking. In: Proc. of CVPR, pp. 758–765 (2006)
3. Brox, T., Bruhn, A., Papenberg, N., Weickert, J.: High accuracy optical flow estimation based on a theory for warping. In: Pajdla, T., Matas, J(G.) (eds.) ECCV 2004. LNCS, vol. 3024, pp. 25–36. Springer, Heidelberg (2004)
4. Brox, T., Rosenhahn, B., Cremers, D., Seidel, H.-P.: High accuracy optical flow serves 3-D pose tracking: Exploiting contour and flow based constraints. In: Leonardis, A., Bischof, H., Pinz, A. (eds.) ECCV 2006. LNCS, vol. 3952, pp. 98–111. Springer, Heidelberg (2006)
5. Kehl, R., Gool, L.V.: Markerless tracking of complex human motions from multiple views. CVIU 104(2), 190–209 (2006)
6. Lowe, D.G.: Distinctive image features from scale-invariant keypoints. IJCV 20, 91–110 (2004)
7. Mikolajczyk, K., Schmid, C.: A performance evaluation of local descriptors. In: Proc. of CVPR, vol. 2, pp. 257–263 (2003)
8. Pebay, P.P., Baker, T.J.: A comparison of triangle quality measures. In: Proceedings to the 10th International Meshing Roundtable, pp. 327–340 (2001)

Chapter 11
Video-Based Performance Capture

In this chapter, by combining the power of surface- and volume-based shape deformation techniques with a novel mesh-based analysis-through-synthesis framework, a new marker-less approach to capture human performances from multi-view video is described. Furthermore, a silhouette rim-based technique and a model-guided multi-view stereo approach are also presented, which enables the acquisition of fine dynamic subtle details more accurately.

In the previous chapters (Chapter 8, 9 and 10), the difficulties of human performance capture have been presented. In general, current methods do not allow for what both actors and directors would prefer: to capture human performances densely in space and time, i.e. to be able to jointly capture accurate dynamic shape, motion and textural appearance of actors in arbitrary everyday apparel.

To bridge this gap, in this chapter, we describe a new marker-less dense performance capture technique that is able to reconstruct motion and spatio-temporally coherent time-varying geometry of a performer moving in his/her normal and even loose or wavy clothing from multiple video streams. Our algorithm jointly delivers time-varying scene geometry with coherent connectivity, accurate time-varying shape detail even of people wearing wide apparel such as skirts, and, being completely passive, enables us to record time-varying surface appearance as well. It thus produces a rich dynamic scene representation which, in particular due to the coherent geometry discretization, can be easily made available to and modified by animators. The method described in this chapter improves over the previous approaches (Chapter 9 and 10) since it allows the acquisition of faster and more complex human performances. Furthermore, fine dynamic subtle details are captured more accurately by combining a silhouette rim-based technique and a model-guided multi-view stereo approach.

The main contribution of the chapter is a new video-based performance capture method [1], which

- passively reconstructs spatio-temporally coherent shape, motion and texture of actors at high quality;

E. de Aguiar: Animation & Performance Capture Using Digi. Models, COSMOS 5, pp. 101–117.
springerlink.com

- draws its strength from an effective combination of a new skeleton-less shape deformation method, a new analysis-through-synthesis framework for pose recovery, and a new model-guided multi-view stereo approach for shape refinement;
- and exceeds capabilities of many previous capture techniques, by allowing the user to record people wearing loose apparel and people performing fast and complex motion.

The remainder of this chapter is structured as follows: Sect. 11.1 briefly describes our efficient performance capture framework. Performances are captured by first employing a new analysis-through-synthesis procedure for global pose alignment in each frame (Sect. 11.2), and thereafter, a model-guided multi-view stereo and a contour alignment method recovers small-scale surface detail, Sect. 11.3. At the end, we present the results, showing that our approach can reliably reconstruct very complex motion, which would even challenge the limits of traditional skeleton-based optical capturing approaches, Sect. 11.4.

11.1 Overview

Prior to capturing human performances, we take a full-body laser scan of the subject in its current apparel by means of a Vitus Smart^{TM} laser scanner. After scanning, the subject immediately moves to the adjacent multi-view recording area, Chapter 4. For each subject and each type of apparel, we record a multitude of different performances. As a pre-processing step, color-based background subtraction is applied to all video footage, yielding silhouette images of the captured performers, Sect. 2.3.1.

Once all of the data has been captured, our automatic performance reconstruction pipeline begins. Our computational model of shape and motion is obtained by first transforming the raw scan into a high-quality surface mesh $\mathcal{M}_{tri} = (V_{tri}, T_{tri})$ (with n_s vertices $V_{tri} = \{v_1 \ldots v_{n_s}\}$ and m_s triangles $T_{tri} = \{t_1 \ldots t_{m_s}\}$) employing the method of [5], see Fig. 11.1(left). Additionally, we create a coarser tetrahedral version of the surface scan $\mathcal{T}_{tet} = (V_{tet}, T_{tet})$ (comprising of n_t vertices V_{tet} and m_t tetrahedrons T_{tet}) by applying a quadric error decimation and a subsequent constrained Delaunay tetrahedralization, Fig. 11.1(right). Typically, M_{tri} contains between 30000 and 40000 triangles, and the corresponding tet-version between 5000 and 6000 tetrahedrons. Both models are automatically registered to the first pose of the actor in the input footage by means of a procedure based on iterative closest points (ICP).

Our capturing framework is designed to meet the difficult challenges imposed by our goal: to capture from sparse multi-view video a spatio-temporally coherent shape, motion, subtlest surface deformation and textural appearance of actors performing fast and complex motion in general apparel. Our method explicitly abandons a skeletal motion parametrization and resorts to deformable models as scene representation. Thereby, we are facing a harder tracking problem, but gain an intriguing advantage: we are now able to track non-rigidly deforming surfaces (like wide clothing) in the same way as rigidly deforming models, and do not require prior assumptions about material distributions or the segmentation of the model.

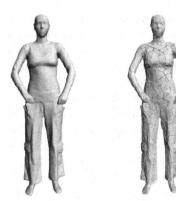

Fig. 11.1 A surface scan $\mathcal{M}_{tri}$ of an actress (**left**) and the corresponding tetrahedral mesh T_{tet} in an exploded view (**right**). [1] ©2008 Association for Computing Machinery, Inc. Reprinted by permission.

The first core algorithmic ingredient of our performance capture framework is a fast and reliable shape deformation framework, that expresses the deformation of the whole model based on a few point handles, Sect. 3.3. The second ingredient is a robust way to infer the motion of the deformation handles from the multi-view video data, Sect. 11.2 and Sect. 11.3. We capture performances in a multi-resolution way to increase reliability. First, an analysis-through-synthesis method based on image and silhouette cues estimates the global pose of an actor at each frame on the basis of the lower-detail tetrahedral input model, Sect. 11.2. Once global poses were found, the low-frequency aspect of the performances, i.e. small-scale time-varying shape details on the surface, are captured. To this end, the global poses are transferred to the high-detail surface scan, and surface shape is refined by enforcing contour alignment and performing model-guided stereo, Sect. 11.3.

The output of our method is a dense representation of the performance in both space and time. It comprises of accurately deformed spatio-temporally coherent geometry that nicely captures the liveliness, motion and shape detail of the original input.

11.2 Capturing the Global Model Pose

Our first step aims at recovering, for each time step of the video, a global pose of the tetrahedral input model that matches the pose of the real actor. Decoupling global pose computation from the estimation of small surfaces makes performance capture a more stable procedure. Consequently, our model representation at this point is the coarse tetrahedral mesh $\mathcal{T}_{tet}$. To modify its pose, we employ the volumetric deformation method, Chapter 3, with its noted advantageous shape preservation properties that facilitate tracking. In a nutshell, our global pose extraction method computes deformation constraints from each pair of subsequent multi-view input video frames at times t and $t + 1$. It then applies the volumetric shape deformation procedure to modify the pose of T_{tet} at time t (that was found previously) until it aligns with the input data at time $t+1$. In order to converge to a plausible pose under this highly multi-modal goodness-of-fit criterion, it is essential that we extract the right types of features from the images in the right sequence and apply the resulting deformation constraints in the correct order.

To serve this purpose, our pose recovery process begins with the extraction of 3D vertex displacements from reliable image features, which brings our model close to its final pose even if scene motion is rapid, Sect. 11.2.1. The distribution of 3D features on the model surface depends on the scene structure, e.g. texture, and can, in general, be non-uniform or sparse. Therefore, the resulting pose may not be entirely correct. Furthermore, potential outliers in the correspondences make additional pose update steps unavoidable. We therefore subsequently resort to two additional steps that exploit silhouette data to fully recover the global pose. The first step refines the shape of the outer model contours until they match the multi-view input silhouette boundaries, Sect. 11.2.2. The second step optimizes 3D displacements of key vertex handles until optimal multi-view silhouette overlap is reached, Sect. 11.2.3. Conveniently, the multi-view silhouette overlap SIL can be quickly computed as an XOR operation on the GPU [3].

We gain further tracking robustness by subdividing the surface of the volume model into a set R of approximately 100-200 regions of similar size during preprocessing [9]. Rather than inferring displacements for each vertex, we determine representative displacements for each region as explained in the following sections.

11.2.1 Pose Initialization from Image Features

Given two sets of multi-view video frames $I_1(t), \ldots, I_k(t)$ and $I_1(t+1), \ldots, I_k(t+1)$ from subsequent time steps, our first processing step extracts SIFT features in each frame [7] (see Fig. 11.2). This yields, for each camera view k and either time step, a list of $\ell(k) = 1, \ldots, L_k$ 2D feature locations $u_{k,t}^{\ell(k)}$ along with their SIFT feature descriptors $dd_{k,t}^{\ell(k)}$ – henceforth we refer to each such list as $LD_{k,t}$. SIFT features are our descriptors of choice, as they are robust against illumination changes and out-of-plane rotation, and enable reliable correspondence finding even if the scene motion is fast.

Let $\mathcal{T}_{tet}(t)$ be the pose of $\mathcal{T}_{tet}$ at time t. To transform feature data into deformation constraints for vertices of $\mathcal{T}_{tet}(t)$, we first need to pair image features from time t with vertices in the model. We therefore first associate each vt_i of $\mathcal{T}_{tet}(t)$ with that descriptor $dd_{k,t}^i$ from each $I_k(t)$ that is located closest to the projected location of vt_i in this respective camera. We perform this computation for all camera views and discard a feature association if vt_i is not visible from k or if the distance between the projected position of vt_i and the image position of $dd_{k,t}^i$ is too large. This way, we obtain a set of associations $A(vt_i,t) = \{dd_{1,t}^{j1}, \cdots, dd_{K,t}^{jK}\}$ for a subset of vertices that contains at most one feature from each camera. Lastly, we check the consistency of each $A(vt_i,t)$ by comparing the pseudo-intersection point p_i^{INT} of the reprojected rays passing through $u_{1,t}^{j1}, \ldots, u_{K,t}^{jK}$ to the 3D position of vt_i in model pose $\mathcal{T}_{tet}(t)$.

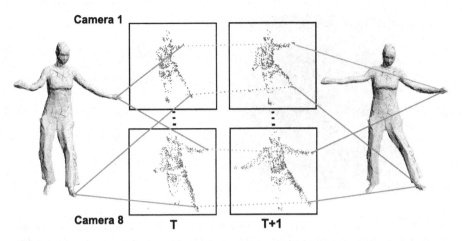

Fig. 11.2 3D correspondences are extracted from corresponding SIFT features in respective input camera views at t and $t + 1$. These 3D correspondences, two of them illustrated by lines, are used to deform the model into a first pose estimate for $t + 1$. [1] ©2008 Association for Computing Machinery, Inc. Reprinted by permission.

If the distance $\|vt_i - p_i^{INT}\|$ is greater than a threshold $\mathscr{E}_{DIST}$, the original feature association is considered implausible and vt_i is removed from the candidate list for deformation handles.

The next step is to establish temporal correspondences, i.e. to find for each vertex vt_i with feature association $A(vt_i, t)$ the corresponding association $A(vt_i, t + 1)$ with features from the next time step. To this end, we preliminarily find for each $dd_{k,t}^j \in A(vt_i, t)$ a descriptor $dd_{k,t+1}^f \in LD_{k,t+1}$ by means of nearest neighbor distance matching in the descriptor values, and add $dd_{k,t+1}^f$ to $A(vt_i, t + 1)$. In practice, this initial assignment is likely to contain outliers, and therefore we compute the final set of temporal correspondences by means of robust spectral matching [6]. This method efficiently bypasses the combinatorial complexity of the correspondence problem by formulating it in closed form as a spectral analysis problem on a graph adjacency matrix. Incorrect matches are eliminated by searching for an assignment in which both the feature descriptor values across time are consistent, and pairwise feature distances across time are preserved. Fig. 11.2 illustrates a subset of associations found for two camera views. From the final set of associations $A(vt_i, t + 1)$, we compute the predicted 3D target position $\mathbf{p}_i^{EST}$ of vertex vt_i again as the virtual intersection point of reprojected image rays through the 2D feature positions.

Each vertex vt_i for which a new estimated position was found is a candidate for a deformation handle. However, we do not straightforwardly apply all handles to move $\mathscr{T}_{tet}$ directly to the new target pose. We rather propose the following stepwise procedure which, in practice, is less likely to converge to implausible model configurations: We resort to the set of regions R on the surface of the tet-mesh (as described above) and find for each region $r_i \in R$ one best handle from all candidate handles that lie in r_i. The best handle vertex vt_i is the one whose local normal

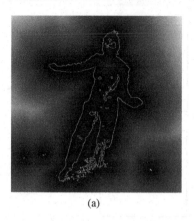

(a)   (b)

Fig. 11.3 (a) Color-coded distance field from the image silhouette contour shown for one camera view. (b) Rim vertices with respect to one camera view marked in red on the tetrahedral model. [1] ©2008 Association for Computing Machinery, Inc. Reprinted by permission.

is most collinear with the difference vector $\mathbf{p}_i^{EST} - v_i$. If no handle is found for a region, we constrain the center of that region to its original 3D position in $\mathcal{T}_{tet}(t)$ which prevents unconstrained surface areas from arbitrary drifting. For each region handle, we define a new intermediate target position as $q_i' = vt_i + \frac{p_i^{EST} - vt_i}{\|p_i^{EST} - vt_i\|}$. Typically, we obtain position constraints q_i' for around 70% to 90% of the surface regions R that are then used to change the pose of the model. This step-wise deformation is repeated until the multi-view silhouette overlap error $SIL(\mathcal{T}_{tet}, t+1)$ cannot be further improved.

In contrast to the method proposed in Chapter 10, we do not require tracking of features across the entire sequence, which greatly contributes to the reliability of this method. The output of this step is a feature-based pose estimate $\mathcal{T}_{tet}^F(t+1)$.

11.2.2 Refining the Pose Using Silhouette Rims

In image regions with sparse or low-frequency textures, only few SIFT features may have been found, which may cause a starkly uneven distribution of deformation handles, or may generate areas with no handles at all. In consequence, the pose of $\mathcal{T}_{tet}^F(t+1)$ may not be correct in all parts. We therefore resort to another constraint that is independent of image texture and has the potential to correct such misalignments. To this end, we derive additional deformation constraints for a subset of vertices on $\mathcal{T}_{tet}^F(t+1)$ that we call *rim vertices* $V_{RIM}(t+1)$, see Fig. 11.3(b). Rim vertices are vertices whose projections lie on the silhouette contour of the performer in at least one $I_k(t+1)$, and whose normals are perpendicular to its viewing direction. By displacing them along their normals until alignment with the respective silhouette boundaries in 2D is reached, we are able to improve the pose accuracy for the model at $t+1$.

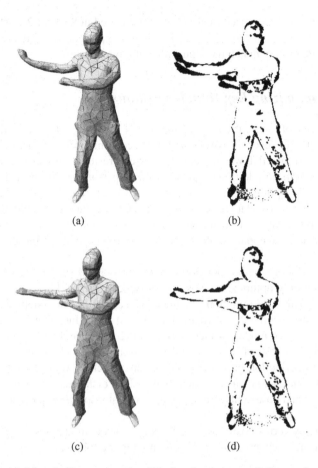

In order to find the elements of $V_{RIM}(t+1)$, we first calculate contour images $C_{k,t+1}$ using the rendered volumetric model silhouettes. A vertex vt_i is considered a rim vertex if it projects into close vicinity of the silhouette contour in (at least) one of the $C_{k,t+1}$, and if the normal of vt_i is perpendicular to the viewing direction of the camera k.

For each element $vt_i \in V_{RIM}(t+1)$ a 3D displacement is computed by analyzing the projected location $u_{k,t+1}$ of the vertex into the camera k that originally defined its rim status. The value of the distance field from the contour at the projected location defines the total displacement length in vertex normal direction, Fig. 11.3(a). This way, we obtain deformation constraints for rim vertices which we apply in the same step-wise deformation procedure that was already used in Sect. 11.2.1. The result is a new model configuration $\mathscr{T}_{tet}^{R}(t+1)$ in which the projections of the outer model contours more closely match the input silhouette boundaries.

11.2.3 Optimizing Key Handle Positions

In the majority of cases, the pose of the model in $\mathscr{T}_{tet}^{R}(t+1)$ is already close to a good match. However, in particular if the scene motion was fast or the initial pose estimate from SIFT was not entirely correct, residual pose errors remain. We therefore perform an additional optimization step that corrects such residual errors by globally optimizing the positions of a subset of deformation handles until good silhouette overlap is reached. Note that for the success of this step, a good pose initialization from the preceding steps is indispensable. Only in their combination all pose update strategies make up a robust analysis-through-synthesis framework.

Instead of optimizing the position of all $1000 - 2000$ vertices of the volumetric model, we only optimize the position of typically 15-25 key vertices $V_k \subset V_{tet}$ until the tetrahedral deformation scheme produces optimal silhouette overlap. We ask the user to specify key vertices manually, a procedure that has to be done only once for every model. Typically, key vertices are marked close to anatomical joints, and in case of model parts representing loose clothing, a simple uniform handle distribution produces good results. Tracking robustness is increased by designing our energy function such that surface distances between key handles are preserved, and pose configurations with low distortion energy E_D are preferred, Sect. 3.3.

Given all key vertex positions $vt_i \in V_k$ in the current model pose $\mathscr{T}_{tet}^{R}(t+1)$, we optimize for their new positions p_i by minimizing the following energy functional:

$$E(V_k) = w_S \cdot SIL(T_{tet}(V_k), t+1) + w_D \cdot E_D + w_C \cdot E_C. \tag{11.1}$$

Here, $SIL(T_{tet}(V_k), t+1)$ denotes the multi-view silhouette overlap error of the tet-mesh in its current deformed pose $T_{tet}(V_k)$, which is defined by the new positions of the V_k. E_D is the deformation energy as defined in Sect. 3.3. Implicitly we reason that low energy configurations are more plausible. E_C penalizes changes in distance between neighboring key vertices. All three terms are normalized and the weights w_S, w_D, and w_C are chosen such that $SIL(T_{tet}(V_k), t+1)$ is the dominant term. In our solution, E_D and E_C are used to regularize the solution avoiding that the distance between neighboring key vertices increases or decreases too much, which creates bad deformations. We use a Quasi-Newton LBFGS-B method to minimize Eq. 11.1 [2].

Fig. 11.4 illustrates the improvements in the new output pose $\mathscr{T}_{tet}^{O}(t+1)$ achieved through key handle optimization. The output of this step is a new configuration of the tetrahedral model $\mathscr{T}_{tet}^{O}(t+1)$ that captures the overall stance of the model and serves as the starting point for the subsequent surface detail capture.

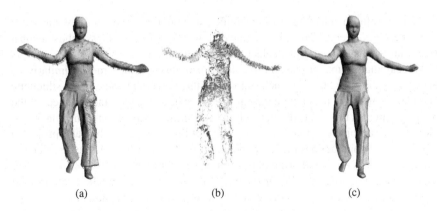

(a)   (b)   (c)

Fig. 11.5 Capturing small-scale surface detail: (**a**) first, deformation constraints from silhouette contours, shown as red arrows, are estimated. (**b**) Additional deformation handles are extracted from a 3D point cloud that was computed via model-guided multi-view stereo. (**c**) Together, both sets of constraints deform the surface scan to a highly accurate pose. [1] ©2008 Association for Computing Machinery, Inc. Reprinted by permission.

11.2.4 Practical Considerations

The above sequence of steps is performed for each pair of subsequent time instants. Surface detail capture, Sect. 11.3, commences after the global poses were found for all frames.

Typically, the rim step described in Sect. 11.2.2 is performed once more after the last silhouette optimization step, which in some cases leads to a better model alignment. We also perform a consistency check on the output of our low frequency pose capture approach to correct potential self-intersections. To this end, for every vertex lying inside another tetrahedron, we use the volumetric deformation method to displace this vertex in outward direction along its normal until the intersection is resolved.

11.3 Capturing Surface Detail

Once global pose has been recovered for each frame, the pose sequence of $\mathcal{T}_{tet}$ is mapped to $\mathcal{M}_{tri}$, Sect. 3.3. In the following section, the process of shape detail capture at a single time step is explained.

11.3.1 Adaptation along Silhouette Contours

In a first step, we adapt the silhouette rims of our fine mesh to better match the input silhouette contours. As we are now working on a surface mesh which is already very close to the correct configuration, we can allow a much broader and less smooth range of deformations than in the volumetric case, and thereby bring the model to much closer alignment with the input data. At the same time, we have to be more careful in selecting our constraints, since noise in the data now has more deteriorating influence. This also means that our deformation is less robust against errors and we have to carefully select the constraints.

We calculate rim vertices for the high-resolution surface mesh similarly to Sect. 11.2.2, Fig. 11.5(a). For each rim vertex, the closest 2D point on the silhouette boundary is found in the camera view that defines its rim status, and we check if the image gradient at the input silhouette point has a similar orientation to the image gradient in the reprojected model contour image. If this is the case, the back-projected input contour point defines the target position for the rim vertex. If the distance between back-projection and original position is smaller than threshold $\mathscr{E}_{RIM}$, we add it as a constraint to Eq. 3.5. We also check if the vertex v_i and the 2D contour point have a similar orientation by comparing their image projected gradients.

We use a low weight w_i for the rim constraint points in Eq. 3.5. This has a regularizing and damping effect on the deformation that minimizes implausible shape adaptation in the presence of noise. After processing all vertices, we solve for the new surface $\mathscr{M}'(t)_{tri}$. This procedure is iterated up to 20 times or until silhouette overlap cannot be further improved.

11.3.2 Model-Guided Multi-view Stereo

Although the silhouette rims only provide reliable constraints on outer boundaries, they are usually evenly distributed on the surface. Hence, the Laplacian-based deformation method in general nicely adapts the shape of the whole model also in areas which do not project on image contours. Unless the surface of the actor has a complicated shape with many concavities, the result of the rim adaptation is already a realistic representation of the correct shape.

However, in order to recover shape details in regions that do not project to silhouette boundaries, such as folds and concavities in a skirt, we resort to photoconsistency information. To serve this purpose, we derive additional deformation constraints by applying the multi-view stereo method proposed by [4]. Since our model is already close to the correct surface, we can initialize the stereo optimization from the current surface estimate and constrain the correlation search to 3D points that are at most ± 2 cm away from $\mathscr{M}(t)_{tri}$.

As we have far less viewpoints of our subject than Goesele et al. [4] and our actors can wear apparel with little texture, the resulting depth maps (one for each input view) are often sparse and noisy. Nonetheless, they provide important additional cues about the object's shape. We merge the depth maps produced by the stereo approach into a single point cloud $\mathscr{P}$, Fig. 11.5(b), and thereafter project points from V_{tri} onto $\mathscr{P}$ using a method similar to [8]. These projected points provide additional position constraints that we can use in conjunction with the rim vertices in the Laplacian-based deformation framework, Eq. 3.5. PV_t give us additional positional constraints to add to the energy minimization from Eq. 3.5 in addition to the rim constraints RV_t. Given the uncertainty in the data, we solve the Laplace system with lower weights for the stereo constraints, Sect. 3.2.2.

Fig. 11.6 A sequence of poses captured from eight video recordings of a capoeira turn kick. Our algorithm delivers spatio-temporally coherent geometry of the moving performer, capturing both the time-varying surface detail as well as details in his motion faithfully. [1] ©2008 Association for Computing Machinery, Inc. Reprinted by permission.

11.4 Results and Discussion

Our test data were recorded in our acquisition setup described in Chapter 4. It comprises of 12 sequences showing four different actors, and feature between 200 and 600 frames each. To show the large application range of our performance capture algorithm, the subjects wore a wide range of different apparel, ranging from tight to loose, and made of fabrics with prominent texture as well as plain colors only. Also, the recovered set of motions ranges from simple walks, over different dance styles, to fast capoeira sequences. As shown in Figs. 11.6, 11.7 and 11.10, our algorithm faithfully reconstructs this wide spectrum of scenes. We would also like to note that, although we focused on human performers, our algorithm would work equally well for animals provided that a laser scan can be acquired.

Fig. 11.6 shows several captured poses of a very rapid capoeira sequence in which the actor performs a series of turn kicks. Despite the fact that in our 24 fps recordings the actor rotates by more than 25 degrees in-between some subsequent frames, both shape and motion are reconstructed with high fidelity. The resulting animation even shows small deformation details such as the waving of the trouser legs. Furthermore, even with the plain white clothing that the actor wears in the input, which exhibits only few traceable SIFT features, our method performs reliably as it can capitalize on rims and silhouettes as additional sources of information. Comparing a single moment from the kick to an input frame confirms the high quality of our reconstruction, Fig. 11.7 (left) (Note that input and virtual camera views differ slightly). Furthermore, Fig. 11.7 (middle) shows that our method is able to capture a fast and fluent jazz dance performance with complicated self-occlusions, such as the inter-twisted arm-motion in front of the torso.

Fig. 11.7(right) and Fig. 11.10 show one of the main strengths of our method, namely its ability to capture the full time-varying shape of a dancing girl wearing a skirt. Even though the skirt is of largely uniform color, our method captures the natural waving and lifelike dynamics of the fabric. The overall body posture and the folds of the skirt were recovered nicely without the user specifying a segmentation of the model beforehand. A visual comparison to the input shows that the captured

Table 11.1 Average run times per frame for individual steps. [1] ©2008 Association for Computing Machinery, Inc. Reprinted by permission.

Step	Time
SIFT step (Sect. 11.2.1)	~5s
Global rim step (Sect. 11.2.2)	~4s
Key handle optimization (Sect. 11.2.3)	~40s
Contour-based refinement (Sect. 11.3.1)	~4s
Stereo, 340 × 340 depth maps (Sect. 11.3.2)	~30s

skirt geometry exhibits the same motion detail and lifelike dynamics as the real skirt, and at the same time, the rest of the body is faithfully captured too. Up to now, other passive methods from the literature have not been able to capture both spatio-temporally coherent shape and motion of such kind of performances. We would also like to note that in these sequences the benefits of the stereo step in recovering concavities are most apparent. In the other test scenes, the effects are less pronounced and we therefore deactivated the stereo step (Sect. 11.3.2) there to reduce computation time. In general, we also smooth the final sequence of vertex positions to remove any remaining temporal noise.

11.4.1 Validation and Discussion

Table 11.1 gives detailed average timings for each individual step in our algorithm. These timings were obtained with a highly unoptimized single-threaded code running on an Intel Core Duo T2500 Laptop with 2.0 GHz. We see plenty of room for implementation improvement, and anticipate that parallelization can lead to a significant run time reduction.

So far, we have visually shown the high capture quality, as well as the large application range and versatility of our approach. To formally validate the accuracy of our method, we have compared the silhouette overlap of our tracked output models with the segmented input frames. We use this criterion since, to our knowledge, there is no gold-standard alternative capturing approach that would provide us with accurate time-varying 3D data. The re-projections of our final results typically overlap with over 85% of the input silhouette pixels, already after global pose capture only (Fig. 11.8(a)). Surface detail capture further improves this overlap to more than 90%. Please note that this measure is slightly negatively biased by errors in foreground segmentation in some frames that appear as erroneous silhouette pixels. Visual inspection of the silhouette overlap therefore confirms the almost perfect alignment of model and actual person silhouette. Fig. 11.8(b) shows a blended overlay between the rendered model and an input frame which proves this point.

Our algorithm robustly handles even noisy input, e.g. due to typically observed segmentation errors in our color-based segmentation. In particular, if foreground colors resemble the background (e.g. black hair in front of a black background in some of our data), color-based segmentation may produce erroneous silhouettes.

Fig. 11.7 (top) One moment from a very fast capoeira turn kick. **(middle)** Jazz dance posture with reliably captured inter-twisted arm motion. **(bottom)** Reconstructed details in the dancing sequence showing a girl wearing a skirt. (Input and virtual viewpoints differ minimally). [1] ©2008 Association for Computing Machinery, Inc. Reprinted by permission.

Nonetheless, our method delivers reliable reconstructions under typically observed segmentation errors. All 12 input sequences were reconstructed fully-automatically after only minimal initial user input. As a pre-processing step, the user marks the head and foot regions of each model to exclude them from surface detail capture. Even slightest silhouette errors in these regions (in particular due to shadows on the floor and black hair color) would otherwise cause unnatural deformations.

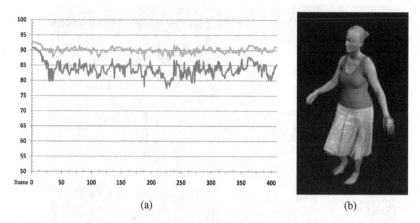

(a)   (b)

Fig. 11.8 Evaluation: per-frame silhouette overlap in per cent after global pose estimation and after surface detail reconstruction (**a**). Blended overlay between an input image and the reconstructed model showing the almost perfect alignment of our performance capture approach (**b**). [1] ©2008 Association for Computing Machinery, Inc. Reprinted by permission.

Furthermore, for each model the user once marks at most 25 deformation handles needed for the key handle optimization step, Sect. 11.2.3.

In individual frames of two out of three capoeira turn kick sequences (11 out of around 1000 frames), as well as in one frame of each of the skirt sequences (2 frames from 850 frames), the output of global pose recovery showed slight misalignments in one of the limbs. Please note that, despite these isolated pose errors, the method always recovers immediately and tracks the whole sequence without drifting – this means the algorithm can run without supervision and the results can be checked afterwards. All observed pose misalignments were exclusively due to oversized silhouette areas because of either motion blur or strong shadows on the floor. Both of this could have been prevented by better adjustment of lighting and shutter speed, and by using more advanced segmentation schemes. In either case of global pose misalignment, at most two deformation handle positions had to be slightly adjusted by the user. In none of the over 3500 input frames we processed in total, it was necessary to manually correct the output of surface detail capture (Sect. 11.3).

Despite our method's large application range, there are a few limitations to be considered. Our current silhouette rim matching may produce erroneous deformations if the topological structure of the input silhouette is too different from the reprojected model silhouette. As our low-frequency adaptation generates a good initialization, which is already close to the actual silhouette, this effect can be overcome by careful selection of parameters. However, in none of our test scenes this turned out to be an issue. Currently, we are recording in a controlled studio environment to obtain good segmentations, but are confident that a more advanced background segmentation will enable us to handle outdoor scenes.

Moreover, there is a resolution limit to our deformation capture. Some of the high-frequency detail in our final result, such as fine wrinkles in clothing or details

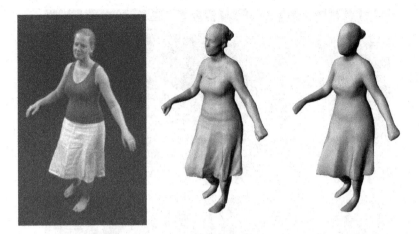

Fig. 11.9 Input frame (**left**) and reconstructions using a detailed (**middle**) and a coarse model (**right**). Although the fine details on the skirt are due to the input laser scan, even with a coarse template, our method captures the folds and the overall lifelike motion of the cloth. [1] ©2008 Association for Computing Machinery, Inc. Reprinted by permission.

of the face, has been part of the laser-scan in the first place. The deformation on this level of detail is not actually captured, but it is "baked in" to the deforming surface. To illustrate the level of detail that we are actually able to reconstruct, we generated a result with a coarse scan that lacks fine surface detail. Fig. 11.9 shows an input frame (left), as well as the reconstructions using the detailed scan (middle) and the coarse model (right). While, as noted before, finest detail in Fig. 11.9 (middle) is due to the high-resolution laser scan, even with a coarse scan, our method still captures the important lifelike motion and the deformation details, Fig. 11.9 (right).

Also, in our system the topology of the input scanned model is preserved over the whole sequence. For this reason, we are not able to track surfaces which arbitrarily change apparent topology over time (e.g. the movement of hair or deep folds with self-collisions). Further on, although we prevent self-occlusions during global pose capture, we currently do not correct them in the output of surface detail capture. However, their occurrence is rather seldom. Manual or automatic correction by collision detection would also be feasible.

Our volume-based deformation technique essentially mimics elastic deformation, thus the geometry generated by the low-frequency tracking may in some cases have a rubbery look. For instance, an arm may not only bend at the elbow, but rather bend along its entire length. Surface detail capture eliminates such artifacts in general, and a more sophisticated yet slower finite element deformation could reduce this problem already at the global pose capture stage.

Despite these limitations, we have presented a new video-based performance capture approach that produces a novel dense and feature-rich output format comprising of spatio-temporally coherent high-quality geometry, lifelike motion data, and optionally the surface texture of recorded actors. By combining an efficient volume- and surface-based deformation schemes, a multi-view analysis-through-synthesis

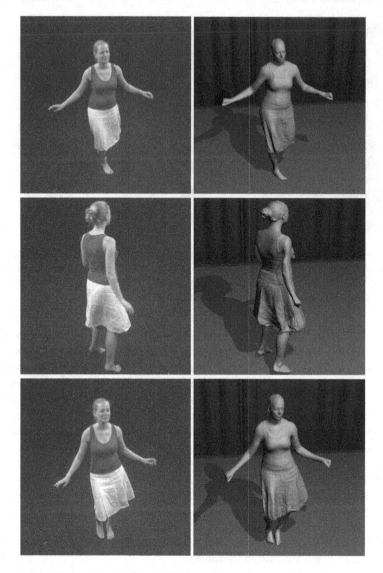

Fig. 11.10 Side-by-side comparison of the input image and the reconstruction of a dancing girl wearing a skirt (input and virtual viewpoints differ minimally). Body pose and detailed geometry of the waving skirt, including lifelike folds and wrinkles visible in the input, have been recovered. [1] ©2008 Association for Computing Machinery, Inc. Reprinted by permission.

procedure, and a multi-view stereo approach, our method is able to reconstruct an unprecedented range of real-world scenes at a high level of detail. The proposed method supplements and exceeds the capabilities of optical capturing systems that are widely used in the industry, and will provide animators and CG artists with a new level of flexibility in acquiring and modifying real-world content.

References

1. de Aguiar, E., Stoll, C., Theobalt, C., Ahmed, N., Seidel, H.P., Thrun, S.: Performance capture from sparse multi-view video. In: ACM TOG, Proc. SIGGRAPH (2008)
2. Byrd, R., Lu, P., Nocedal, J., Zhu, C.: A limited memory algorithm for bound constrained optimization. SIAM J. Sci. Comp. 16(5), 1190–1208 (1995)
3. Carranza, J., Theobalt, C., Magnor, M., Seidel, H.P.: Free-viewpoint video of human actors. ACM TOG (Proc. of SIGGRAPH 2003) 22(3), 569–577 (2003)
4. Goesele, M., Curless, B., Seitz, S.M.: Multi-view stereo revisited. In: Proc. CVPR, pp. 2402–2409 (2006)
5. Kazhdan, M., Bolitho, M., Hoppe, H.: Poisson surface reconstruction. In: Proc. SGP, pp. 61–70 (2006)
6. Leordeanu, M., Hebert, M.: A spectral technique for correspondence problems using pairwise constraints. In: Proc. ICCV, pp. 1482–1489 (2005)
7. Lowe, D.G.: Object recognition from local scale-invariant features. In: Proc. of ICCV, pp. 1150–1157 (1999)
8. Stoll, C., Karni, Z., Rössl, C., Yamauchi, H., Seidel, H.P.: Template deformation for point cloud fitting. In: Symposium on Point-Based Graphics, pp. 27–35 (2006)
9. Yamauchi, H., Gumhold, S., Zayer, R., Seidel, H.P.: Mesh segmentation driven by gaussian curvature. Visual Computer 21(8-10), 649–658 (2005)

Chapter 12
High-Quality 3D Videos

In this chapter, we describe a method to render realistic 3D Videos by applying a clever dynamic 3D texturing scheme to the moving geometry representation captured by the methods proposed in the previous chapters. By displaying high-quality renderings of the recorded actor from any viewpoint, our system enables new interesting applications for 3D Television.

In recent years, an increasing research interest in the field of 3D Video processing has been observed. The goal is to render a real-world scene from arbitrary novel viewpoints photo-realistically. Since the human actor is presumably the most important element of many real-world scenes, the analysis of motion and shape of humans from video, as well as their convincing graphical rendition is required, which is still a challenging task.

In the traditional model-based approach to 3D Video, the motion of a simplified body model is first estimated from multiple video streams [4, 3], and during rendering, it is textured using the input footage. Although these methods deliver realistic free-viewpoint renderings of virtual actors, we expect that a more accurate underlying geometry increases realism even further.

By combining the detailed captured human performances, using any of the methods presented in Chapters 9, 10, or 11, with the multi-view projective texture method proposed in [3], convincing renditions of human actors from arbitrary synthetic viewpoints can be generated in real-time. Due to the highly-detailed underlying scene geometry, the visual results are much better than previous model-based or shape from silhouette-based 3D Video methods, Sect. 8.1.3. In addition, since our performance capture methods generate a natural and time-consistent geometry, 3D Video applications that until now would require a lot of effort are simplified, e.g. 3D Video editing and 3D Video compositing. For example, one can generate multiple single 3D Video scenes, which afterwards could easily be edited and composed together in order to create new sequences.

The main contribution of this chapter is a

- system combining a detailed dynamic scene representation with a projective texture method, enabling realistic renditions of human subjects from arbitrary synthetic viewpoints [1].

E. de Aguiar: Animation & Performance Capture Using Digi. Models, COSMOS 5, pp. 119–124.
springerlink.com

In this chapter, we first describe a dynamic multi-view texturing method, Sect. 12.1. Thereafter, Sect. 12.2 presents the results obtained with our 3D Video system, showing the captured real world scenes from novel synthetic camera perspectives.

12.1 Creating 3D Videos

By combining any of the three previous performance capture methods described in this book, the motion, dynamic shape, and texture information from moving subjects is acquired. This data can be used to create and render convincing free-viewpoint videos that reproduce the omni-directional appearance of the actor. Since no markers are needed to capture the scene, time-varying video footage is available and lifelike surface appearance can be generated using the projective texturing technique described in [3].

In order to display the model, the color of each rendered pixel $c(j)$ is determined by blending all k input multi-view video images I_i according to

$$c(j) = \sum_{i=1}^{k} v_i(j)\omega_i(j)I_i(j) \tag{12.1}$$

where $\omega_i(j)$ denotes the blending weight of camera i and $v_i(j) = \{0,1\}$ is the local visibility. During texture pre-processing, the weights are calculated and the product $v_i(j)\omega_i(j)$ is normalized to ensure energy conservation.

Technically, Eq. 12.1 can be evaluated for each fragment on the GPU, and the rasterization engine interpolates the blending values from the triangle vertices. By this means, time-varying cloth folds and creases, shadows, and facial expressions are faithfully reproduced, leading to a very natural, dynamic appearance of the rendered object.

Blending Weights

The blending weights determine the contribution of each input camera image to the final color of a surface point. If surface reflectance can be assumed to be approximately Lambertian, view-dependent reflection effects play no significant role, and high-quality renditions can be obtained by blending the video images intelligently. Let θ_i denote the angle between a vertex normal and the optical axis of camera i. By emphasizing the camera view with the smallest angle θ_i for each vertex, i.e. the camera that views the vertex most head-on, a consistent, detail-preserving texture is obtained.

Following [3], a visually convincing weight assignment has been found to be

$$\omega_i = \frac{1}{(1 + \max_j(1/\theta_j) - 1/\theta_i)^\alpha}. \tag{12.2}$$

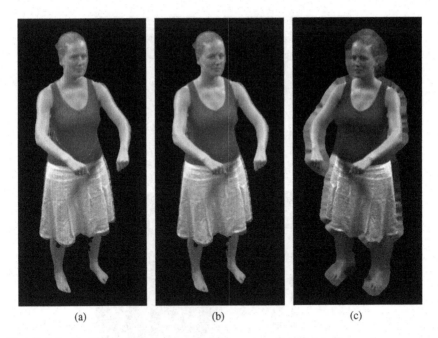

(a)	(b)	(c)

Fig. 12.1 Small differences between object silhouette and model outline causes erroneous texture projections (**a**) that can be corrected by applying an extended soft shadowing method (**b**). Morphologically dilated segmented input video frames can be used to improve projective texturing (**c**).

The parameter α determines the influence of a vertex orientation with respect to the camera viewing directions and consequently the impact of the most head-on camera view per vertex. Singularities are avoided by clamping the value of $1/\theta_i$ to a maximal value. Additionally, the weights ω_i are normalized to sum up to one.

Visibility

Unfortunately, in projective texturing, occlusions are not taken into account and hidden surfaces can be erroneous textured. However, the z-buffer test can be used to determine for every time step which regions are visible from each camera view. Due to inaccuracies in the geometry model, it can happen that the silhouette outlines in the images do not correspond exactly to the outline of the model. As a result, when projecting video images onto the model, a texture seam belonging to some frontal body part may fall into another body part farther back, Fig. 12.1(a).

To avoid such artifacts, extended soft shadowing is applied. For each camera view, all object regions of zero visibility are determined not only from the actual position of the camera, but also from several slightly displaced virtual camera positions. Each vertex is tested whether it is visible from all camera positions. A triangle

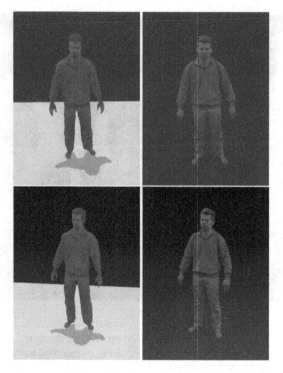

Fig. 12.2 Free-viewpoint renditions with high-quality geometry models. Due to the accurate geometry, the rendered appearance of the actor (**left sub-images**) nicely corresponds to his true appearance in the real world (**right sub-images**). Reprinted from [2] © 2007 IEEE.

is textured by a camera image only if all of its three vertices are completely visible from that camera, Fig. 12.1(b).

Furthermore, to reduce rendering artifacts caused by small segmented silhouette outlines, all image silhouettes are expanded by a couple of pixels prior to rendering. Using a morphological filter operation, the subject's outline in all video images is dilated by copying the silhouette boundary pixel values to adjacent background pixel positions, Fig. 12.1(c).

12.2 Results and Discussion

By coupling our performance capture methods with the texturing approach described in this chapter, realistic 3D Videos can be displayed in real-time. Fig. 12.2 shows two free-viewpoint renditions of a dynamically textured animated model in comparison to the original images of the subject. The free-viewpoint renditions reflect the true appearance of the actor, confirming that the virtual viewpoint renditions look very lifelike. Since we are given a better surface geometry, texture blending artifacts are hardly observed. Furthermore, we can even reproduce the true shape of the sweater which would not have been possible with a coarse template model [3].

Fig. 12.3 (top-middle) High-quality renditions showing a female dancer wearing a skirt and (**bottom**) renditions of a male actor performing a fast and complex capoeira turn kick. The time-varying refined geometry acquired by our previous performance capture approaches leads to a better visual quality. [1] ©2008 Association for Computing Machinery, Inc. Reprinted by permission.

We have created 3D Videos from a variety of scenes ranging from simple walking sequences over dancing moves to complex and expressive capoeira turn kicks. Fig. 12.3 displays renditions showing the female dancer wearing a skirt and the male actor performing a fast and complex turn kick. These sequences are ideal test cases to validate the high-quality of the generated 3D Videos as they exhibit rapid and complex rigid and non-rigid motions. Another advantage of our scheme is that it allows a contiguous surface parameterization of the model, which facilitates higher-level processing operations, as they are needed for 3D Video editing or in reflectance estimation techniques [5, 6]

Although clever texture blending can mask most geometry inaccuracies if a coarse geometry is used, combining a dynamically refined shape representation, acquired by our previous performance capture approaches, leads to an even better visual quality. Improvements in the renderings are due to the improved geometry and, consequently, less surface blending errors during projective texturing are generated. This combination enables high-quality reconstruction of human actors completely passively, and opens the door for attacking new challenging reconstruction problems that were hard due to the lack of a decent dynamic scene capture technology.

References

1. de Aguiar, E., Stoll, C., Theobalt, C., Ahmed, N., Seidel, H.P., Thrun, S.: Performance capture from sparse multi-view video. In: ACM TOG, Proc. SIGGRAPH (2008)
2. de Aguiar, E., Zayer, R., Theobalt, C., Magnor, M., Seidel, H.P.: Video-driven animation of human body scans. In: IEEE 3DTV Conference (2007)
3. Carranza, J., Theobalt, C., Magnor, M., Seidel, H.P.: Free-viewpoint video of human actors. ACM TOG (Proc. of SIGGRAPH 2003) 22(3), 569–577 (2003)
4. Starck, J., Hilton, A.: Towards a 3D virtual studio for human appearance capture. In: Proc. of Vision, Video and Graphics, pp. 17–24 (2003)
5. Theobalt, C., Ahmed, N., de Aguiar, E., Ziegler, G., Lensch, H.P.A., Magnor, M., Seidel, H.P.: Joint motion and reflectance capture for creating relightable 3d videos. Technical Report MPI-I-2005-4-004, MPII. Saarbruecken, Germany (2005)
6. Theobalt, C., Ahmed, N., Lensch, H., Magnor, M., Seidel, H.P.: Seeing people in different light - joint shape, motion, and reflectance capture. IEEE TVCG 13(4), 663–674 (2007)

Part IV
Processing Mesh Animations

Chapter 13
Problem Statement and Preliminaries

In this part of the book, we propose two novel techniques to simplify the process of mesh animations. First, an automatic method to extract a plausible kinematic skeleton, skeletal motion parameters, and surface skinning weights from arbitrary mesh animations is presented. Thereafter, a method to automatically transform mesh animations into animation collages, i.e. moving assemblies of shape primitives from a database, is described.

It has become increasingly popular to create, edit and represent animations not by means of a classical skeleton-based model, but in the form of deforming mesh sequences. The reason for this new trend is that novel mesh deformation methods, as the ones presented in Chapter 3, as well as new surface based scene capture techniques, like the methods presented in the third part of the book, offer a great level of flexibility during animation creation. However, unfortunately the resulting scene representation is less compact than skeletal ones and there is not yet a rich toolbox available which enables easy post-processing and modification of mesh animations.

Animators are used to a large repertoire of tools for editing and rendering traditional skeletal animations, but yet lack the same set of tools for working with mesh-based dynamic scene representations. The method proposed in Chapter 14 bridges this gap, enabling the fully-automatic conversion of a mesh animation into a skeleton-based animation, that can be edited with off-the-shelf tools.

A second novel application is described in Chapter 15. Frequently, researchers in computer graphics aim at developing algorithms that enable the computer and even unexperienced users to reproduce the look of certain styles of visual arts. The proposed system brings together the traditional art form of a collage with the most prominent art form in computer graphics, namely 3D animation, allowing the computer artist to automatically convert her favorite mesh animation into a moving assembly of 3D shape primitives from a database.

In summary, the main contributions of this part of the book are

- a motion-driven mesh segmentation method [3];

E. de Aguiar: Animation & Performance Capture Using Digi. Models, COSMOS 5, pp. 127–132.
springerlink.com

- an algorithm to fully-automatic extract a skeleton structure, skeletal motion parameters, and surface skinning weights from arbitrary deforming mesh sequences [3];
- a system to create animation collages from mesh animations, generating a complete reassembly of the original animation in a new abstract visual style that imitates the spatio-temporal shape and deformation of the input [38].

This chapter proceeds with a review of closely related work in Sect. 13.1. Thereafter, in the following chapters, our two novel approaches to process mesh animations are described in Chapter 14 and Chapter 15. We believe that our new methods are important contributions to the animator's toolbox with a variety of applications in visual arts, animated movie production, and game productions.

13.1   Related Work

In our projects, we jointly solve a variety of algorithmic subproblems by extending ideas from different research areas. In the following sections, we highlight selected related papers from these research categories.

13.1.1   Motion-Driven Mesh Segmentation

Segmenting a static mesh in meaningful parts is an active field of research [34]. However, recently researchers started to also exploit temporal information in mesh animations to create level of detail [35], to improve compression [24, 23, 32], to motion-decompose mesh animations for fast ray-tracing [12], and to cluster triangles in mesh animations for fast rendering [15]. Unfortunately, these methods may generate segments that are not spatially and temporally consistent, i.e. they do not correspond to underlying kinematic hierarchies and are not guaranteed to be spatially connected.

Most recently, [33] proposed a method for extracting a hierarchical, rigid skeleton from a set of example poses, that can also be used for motion-driven segmentation. The main difference to a segmentation method that we propose in the next chapter is the fact that we robustly segment the model by means of spectral clustering. This gives us much greater flexibility, as we can produce segmentations at different user-controlled levels of detail, or automatically detect the optimal number of clusters.

13.1.2   Skeleton Reconstruction

Different ways for performing skeleton extraction, each of them tailored to a specific data type and application, have been proposed in the literature. Some approaches extract skeletons from static meshes to hierarchically decompose the shape [26], to segment the mesh in meaningful regions [16], to gain information on the model's topology [36], and to perform simple mesh editing operations [27, 44, 39]. Thus, extraction of an animation skeleton is not the goal.

The accurate extraction of kinematically and biologically plausible animation skeletons is of great importance in optical motion capture, where the skeletal structure needs to be inferred from marker trajectories [21, 2] or shape-from-silhouette volumes [1]. Similarly, kinematic skeletons can be reconstructed from a set of range scans of humans [4], from CT scans of the human hand [22], from a static surface mesh of a known character [5], or from pose examples [33].

In contrast, the approach proposed in Chapter 14 makes use of entire motion sequences to extract kinematic hierarchies more robustly. It creates a plausible animation skeleton that best explains the data and that closely resembles a skeleton designed by an animator, in case such a skeleton exists for the data set.

13.1.3 Character Skinning

Skinning (also called enveloping) maps the articulated motion of the skeleton to deformations of the character's surface. Due to its efficiency, ease of implementation, and support in many commercial packages, the most widely used method is linear blend skinning [25], where vertex transformations are expressed as weighted linear combinations of bone transformations. Unfortunately, standard linear blending has limited modeling power and cannot reliably reproduce certain effects, such as muscle bulging. Recent blending schemes look at several example poses and suggest methods to overcome the limitations inherent to linear blending by using multi-linear blending weights [43], additional bones to increase reconstruction faithfulness [28], or affine transformations to calculate the deformations [15]. More recently, an improved example-based method has been proposed by [22] and augmented with a GPU approach [31].

In general, the former approaches offer a great level of realism, but are limited by the number of input examples. Alternatively, advanced skinning techniques can also be used to remove some artifacts of the traditional linear method, such as direct quaternion blending [13], spherical blending [18], log-matrix blending [9], or dual quaternion skinning [17].

In a different line of thinking, researchers recently suggested to use the motion of a kinematic skeleton to express constraints for a surface deformation method like a Laplacian deformation [47] or a Poisson deformation [42]. By this means, convincing animations can be obtained as one can capitalize on the full modeling flexibility of a more complex mesh deformation approach.

The skinning method that we detail in the next chapter is closely related to the one proposed in [7], where the skeleton fitted to a static model is used to automatically compute the skinning weights. However, in contrast to their method, the proposed approach uses an entire sequence of mesh poses and extracted skeletons to improve the estimation of the skinning weights.

13.1.4 Editing Mesh Animations

Similar in spirit to our algorithm are methods that manipulate a mesh animation directly based on the spatio-temporal mesh editing operators [46, 20]. While the flexibility of these methods is very high and the resulting edited animations are of high visual quality, they require a fundamental redesign of existing animation tools and do not allow data compression. In particular, when the mesh animation can be explained by a skeleton, transforming a mesh animation into a skeletal one is advantageous, as it enables fast and easy post-processing using the full spectrum of already existing software.

A first step in this direction was taken in [33] where a skeleton and its skinning weights are estimated from a set of example poses. The main differences to the method described in Chapter 14 is that we exploit the full motion information in the input to robustly learn a skeleton by means of spectral clustering, that we get a full range of skeletal motion parameters for the input animation which gives us greater flexibility during post-processing, and that we fit our skinning weights to the entire range of animation frames leading to more reliable estimates.

13.1.5 Shape Matching

The fitting of static shapes to generic primitives, like ellipsoids or general quadrics, has been widely used in geometry processing for efficient data transmission [8], medical visualization [6], or segmentation and piecewise shape approximation [45] in reverse engineering. Alternatively, if the application is bound to work with given primitives, 3D shape matching techniques can also be employed [40, 37].

Global shape matching approaches compare different shapes based on numerical descriptors such as shape distributions [30], Fourier descriptors [41], moment invariants [10, 29], or spherical harmonics [19]. Local shape matching can also be used to identify correspondences between subparts of shapes using artificial surface features [11] or topology graph-based alignment [14].

In our work on animation collages, Chapter 15, we have developed a novel spatio-temporal matching approach based on spherical harmonic descriptors [19], which is more robust and provides a more compact representation to describe the shapes in our time-dependent matching problem.

References

1. de Aguiar, E., Theobalt, C., Magnor, M., Theisel, H., Seidel, H.P.: M3: Marker-free model reconstruction and motion tracking from 3d voxel data. In: Proc. of PG, pp. 101–110 (2004)
2. de Aguiar, E., Theobalt, C., Seidel, H.-P.: Automatic learning of articulated skeletons from 3D marker trajectories. In: Bebis, G., Boyle, R., Parvin, B., Koracin, D., Remagnino, P., Nefian, A., Meenakshisundaram, G., Pascucci, V., Zara, J., Molineros, J., Theisel, H., Malzbender, T. (eds.) ISVC 2006. LNCS, vol. 4291, pp. 485–494. Springer, Heidelberg (2006)
3. de Aguiar, E., Theobalt, C., Thrun, S., Seidel, H.P.: Automatic conversion of mesh animations into skeleton-based animations. Computer Graphics Forum (Proc. Eurographics EG 2008) 27(2), 389–397 (2008)

4. Anguelov, D., Koller, D., Pang, H., Srinivasan, P., Thrun, S.: Recovering articulated object models from 3d range data. In: Proc. of UAI, pp. 18–26 (2004)
5. Aujay, G., Hétroy, F., Lazarus, F., Depraz, C.: Harmonic skeleton for realistic character animation. In: SCA 2007, pp. 151–160 (2007)
6. Banégas, F., Jaeger, M., Michelucci, D., Roelens, M.: The ellipsoidal skeleton in medical applications. In: ACM Solid Modeling and Applications, pp. 30–38 (2001)
7. Baran, I., Popović, J.: Automatic rigging and animation of 3d characters. ACM Trans. Graph. 26(3), 72 (2007)
8. Bischoff, S., Kobbelt, L.: Ellipsoid decomposition of 3D-model. In: IEEE 3DPVT, pp. 480–489 (2002)
9. Cordier, F., Magnenat-Thalmann, N.: A data-driven approach for real-time clothes simulation. Computer Graphics Forum 24, 173–183 (2005)
10. Elad, M., Tal, A., Ar, S.: Content based retrieval of vrml objects: an iterative and interactive approach. In: Proc. Eurographics Workshop on Multimedia 2001, pp. 107–118 (2002)
11. Gal, R., Cohen-Or, D.: Salient geometric features for partial shape matching and similarity. ACM TOG 25(1), 130–150 (2006)
12. Günther, J., Friedrich, H., Wald, I., Seidel, H.P., Slusallek, P.: Ray tracing animated scenes using motion decomposition. Computer Graphics Forum (Proc. Eurographics) 25(3), 517–525 (2006)
13. Hejl, J.: Hardware skinning with quaternions. Game Programming Gems 4, 487–495 (2004)
14. Hilaga, M., Shinagawa, Y., Kohmura, T., Kunii, T.L.: Topology matching for fully automatic similarity estimation of 3d shapes. ACM TOG (Proc. SIGGRAPH), 203–212 (2001)
15. James, D., Twigg, C.: Skinning mesh animations. ACM Transactions on Graphics (Proc. SIGGRAPH) 24(3) (2005)
16. Katz, S., Tal, A.: Hierarchical mesh decomposition using fuzzy clustering and cuts. In: SIGGRAPH 2003, pp. 954–961 (2003)
17. Kavan, L., Collins, S., Zara, J., O'Sullivan, C.: Skinning with dual quaternions. In: ACM SIGGRAPH Symposium on Interactive 3D Graphics and Games, pp. 39–46 (2007)
18. Kavan, L., Žára, J.: Spherical blend skinning: a real-time deformation of articulated models. In: I3D 2005, pp. 9–16 (2005)
19. Kazhdan, M., Funkhouser, T., Rusinkiewicz, S.: Rotation invariant spherical harmonic representation of 3d shape descriptors. In: Proc. SGP, pp. 156–164 (2003)
20. Kircher, S., Garland, M.: Editing arbitrarily deforming surface animations. In: SIGGRAPH 2006, pp. 1098–1107 (2006)
21. Kirk, A.G., O'Brien, J.F., Forsyth, D.A.: Skeletal parameter estimation from optical motion capture data. In: CVPR, pp. 782–788 (2005)
22. Kurihara, T., Miyata, N.: Modeling deformable human hands from medical images. In: SCA 2004, pp. 355–363 (2004)
23. Lee, T.Y., Lin, P.H., Yan, S.U., Lin, C.H.: Mesh decomposition using motion information from animation sequences: Animating geometrical models. Comput. Animat. Virtual Worlds 16(3-4), 519–529 (2005)
24. Lengyel, J.E.: Compression of time-dependent geometry. In: Proc. I3D, pp. 89–95 (1999)
25. Lewis, J.P., Cordner, M., Fong, N.: Pose space deformation: a unified approach to shape interpolation and skeleton-driven deformation. In: Proc. of ACM SIGGRAPH 2000, pp. 165–172 (2000)
26. Lien, J.M., Keyser, J., Amato, N.M.: Simultaneous shape decomposition and skeletonization. In: SPM 2006, pp. 219–228 (2006)

27. Liu, P.C., Wu, F.C., Ma, W.C., Liang, R.H., Ouhyoung, M.: Automatic animation skeleton construction using repulsive force field. In: PG 2003 (2003)
28. Mohr, A., Gleicher, M.: Building efficient, accurate character skins from examples. In: SIGGRAPH 2003, pp. 562–568 (2003)
29. Novotni, M., Klein, R.: 3d zernike descriptors for content based shape retrieval. In: Proc. ACM Symp. on Solid Modeling, pp. 216–225 (2003)
30. Osada, R., Funkhouser, T., Chazelle, B., Dobkin, D.: Matching 3d models with shape distributions. In: Proc. Shape Modeling International, pp. 154–166 (2001)
31. Rhee, T., Lewis, J., Neumann, U.: Real-time weighted pose-space deformation on the gpu. Computer Graphics Forum 25, 439–448 (2006)
32. Sattler, M., Sarlette, R., Klein, R.: Simple and efficient compression of animation sequences. In: Proc. SCA, pp. 209–217 (2005)
33. Schaefer, S., Yuksel, C.: Example-based skeleton extraction. In: SGP 2007, pp. 153–162 (2007)
34. Shamir, A.: A survey on mesh segmentation techniques. Computer Graphics Forum (2008)
35. Shamir, A., Pascucci, V.: Temporal and spatial level of details for dynamic meshes. In: VRST 2001, pp. 77–84 (2001)
36. Sharf, A., Lewiner, T., Shamir, A., Kobbelt, L.: On–the–fly curve-skeleton computation for 3d shapes. Eurographics, 323–328 (2007)
37. Tangelder, J.W., Veltkamp, R.C.: A survey of content based 3d shape retrieval methods. In: Int. Conf. on Shape Modeling and Applications, pp. 145–156 (2004)
38. Theobalt, C., Rössl, C., de Aguiar, E., Seidel, H.P.: Animation collage. In: SCA 2007, pp. 271–280 (2007)
39. Tierny, J., Vandeborre, J., Daoudi, M.: 3d mesh skeleton extraction using topological and geometrical analyses. In: PG 2006, pp. 409–413 (2006)
40. Veltkamp, R.C., Hagedoorn, M.: State of the art in shape matching. In: Conference on Principles of Visual Information Retrieval, pp. 87–119 (2001)
41. Vranic, D.V., Saupe, D., Richter, J.: Tools for 3d-object retrieval: Karhunen-loeve transform and spherical harmonics. In: IEEE MMSP, pp. 293–298 (2001)
42. Wang, R.Y., Pulli, K., Popović, J.: Real-time enveloping with rotational regression. ACM Trans. Graph. 26(3), 73 (2007)
43. Wang, X.C., Phillips, C.: Multi-weight enveloping: Least-squares approximation techniques for skin animation. In: SCA 2002, pp. 129–138 (2002)
44. Wu, F.C., Ma, W.C., Liang, R.H., Chen, B., Ouhyoung, M.: Domain connected graph: the skeleton of a closed 3d shape for animation. Vis. Comput. 22(2), 117–135 (2006)
45. Wu, J., Kobbelt, L.: Structure recovery via hybrid variational surface approximation. Comp. Graphics Forum (Proc. Eurographics) 24, 277–284 (2005)
46. Xu, W., Zhou, K., Yu, Y., Tan, Q., Peng, Q., Guo, B.: Gradient domain editing of deforming mesh sequences. ACM TOG 26(3), 84 (2007)
47. Yoshizawa, S., Belyaev, A.G., Seidel, H.P.: Skeleton-based variational mesh deformations. In: Eurographics, pp. 255–264 (2007)

Chapter 14
Reconstructing Fully-Rigged Characters

In this chapter, we propose a method to automatically extract a plausible kinematic skeleton, skeletal motion parameters, and surface skinning weights from arbitrary mesh animations, bridging the gap between the mesh-based and the skeletal paradigms. By this means, sequences captured in the previous chapters can be automatically transformed into fully-rigged virtual characters.

As mentioned in Chapter 13, a great level of flexibility during animation creation can be achieved by representing animations not by means of a classical skeleton-based model, but in the form of deforming mesh sequences. This is demonstrated in the part III of the book, where we described algorithms to perform mesh-based performance capture. However, until now there is not yet a large amount of methods available which enables easy post-processing and compression of mesh animations.

Xu et al. [20] propose to close this gap by introducing a set of mesh-based operations to post-process surface animations in a similar manner as kinematic representations. Although their method allows for flexible post-processing of time-varying surfaces, it requires a fundamental redesign of existing animation tools and also does not explore data compression possibilities. The latter was the focus of the work by James et al. [9] who aim at extracting a skinning representation from mesh sequences that is well-suited for rendering on graphics hardware but not meant to be used for editing.

In contrast, in this chapter, we propose a method that enables the fully-automatic conversion of an arbitrary mesh animation into a skeleton-based animation. By this means, deforming mesh sequences are transformed into fully-rigged virtual subjects. The original input can then be quickly rendered based on the new compact bone and skin representation or modified using the full repertoire of already existing animation tools.

Given as input a deforming mesh sequence with constant surface connectivity (e.g. captured by the methods described in part III), our algorithm first extracts a plausible kinematic bone hierarchy that closely resembles a skeleton hand-crafted by an animator, Sect. 14.2. Thereafter, our algorithm automatically infers joint motion parameters, Sect. 14.3 and Sect. 14.4, and estimates appropriate surface skinning weights to attach the skeleton to the surface, Sect. 14.5. The output of

E. de Aguiar: Animation & Performance Capture Using Digi. Models, COSMOS 5, pp. 133–148.

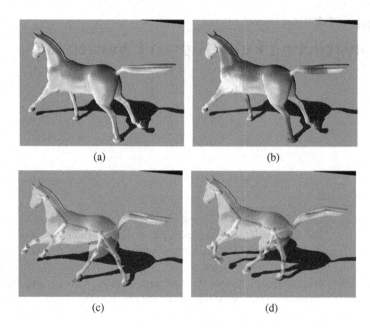

(a)   (b)

(c)   (d)

Fig. 14.1 Overview: **(a)** Input animation, **(b)** color-coded distribution of blending weights, and **(c,d)** two poses of the input re-generated based on our skeleton-based version. Reprinted from [2] © Wiley-Blackwell.

our algorithm is a fully-rigged skeletal version of the original surface-based input. We exemplify the performance of our algorithm by applying it to a variety of hand-crafted and captured sequences, and also prove the faithfulness of the reconstructed skeletal representations to the ground truth input in Sect. 14.6.

In summary, the main contributions of this chapter is an algorithm [2] that

- enables fully-automatic extraction of skeleton structure, skeletal motion parameters and surface skinning weights from arbitrary deforming mesh sequences, and
- thereby enables easy post-processing and fast rendering of mesh animations with standard skeleton-based tools without having to modify them.

As opposed to related methods, Sect 13.1, our approach jointly produces a compact and easily modifiable skeletal version (Fig. 14.1), enables fast and accurate rendering of the original input, enables easy generation of new pose sequences for the input subject, and achieves all this without requiring any modification to already existing animation tools.

14.1 Overview

An overview of our approach is shown in Fig. 14.2. The input to our algorithm is an animated mesh sequence comprising of N frames. We represent an animated mesh

Fig. 14.2 Overview of our algorithm: using an animated mesh as input, our approach segments the model into plausible approximately rigid surface patches, estimates the kinematic skeleton and its motion parameters, and calculates the skinning weights connecting the skeleton to the mesh. The output is a skeleton-based version of the input mesh animation. Reprinted from [2] © Wiley-Blackwell.

sequence by a mesh model $\mathcal{M}_{tri} = (V_{tri}, T_{tri})$ and position data $p_t(v_j) = (x_j, y_j, z_j)_t$ for each vertex $v_j \in V_{tri}$ at all time steps t.

In the first step of our algorithm, we employ spectral clustering to group seed vertices on the mesh into approximately rigid segments. By using the clustered seed vertices we are able to segment the moving mesh into kinematically meaningful approximately rigid patches, Sect. 14.2. Thereafter, adjacent body parts are determined and the topology of the kinematic structure of the mesh is found, Sect. 14.3. Using the estimated topology, joint positions between interconnecting segments are calculated over time. In order to eliminate temporal bone length variations due to per-time step fitting inaccuracies, joint positions are updated at all time steps and an inverse kinematics approach is applied to determine the subject's joint parameters over time, Sect. 14.4. In a last step, we calculate appropriate skinning weights to attach the learned skeleton to the surface, Sect. 14.5. This way, we produce a complete skeleton-based new version of the original input.

14.2 Motion-Driven Segmentation

The first step of our algorithm segments the animated input mesh (given by $\mathcal{M}_{tri}$ and P_t) into spatially coherent patches that undergo approximately the same rigid transformations over time. We initialize our approach by selecting a subset of l vertices that are distributed evenly over the mesh, Fig. 14.3(left). For the selection of the seeds we only consider a reference pose P_{tr} (typically $tr = 0$), and employ a curvature-based segmentation method [21] to decompose the model into l surface patches. The seed vertices are chosen as the vertices closest to the centers of the patches. We typically choose l to be in the range of $0.3 - 1.0\%$ of the total vertex count of the model, which enables reasonably fast decomposition of even large meshes.

Similar to [12, 1] in the context of optical motion capture, the motion trajectories of the seed vertices throughout the whole sequence form the input to a spectral clustering approach [16] which automatically groups the l seeds into k approximately

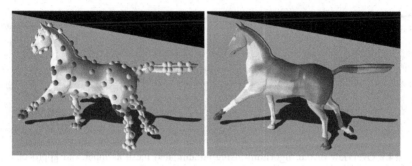

Fig. 14.3 (left) Subset of vertices distributed evenly over the mesh and **(right)** resulting approximately rigid surface patches. Reprinted from [2] © Wiley-Blackwell.

rigidly moving groups. We capitalize on the invariant that mutual distances between points on the same rigid part should only exhibit a small variance while the mesh is moving. After clustering the vertices with similar motion, we transform them into rigidly moving coherent triangle patches.

In order to use spectral clustering, we first construct a spatial affinity matrix A. We developed an affinity criterion specifically for our setting that defines the entries of A as follows:

$$A_{i,j} = e^{-\frac{\sigma_{i,j}+\sqrt{\rho_{i,j}}}{s^2}}, \tag{14.1}$$

where $\rho_{i,j} = \frac{1}{N^2}\sum_t \delta(v_i, v_j, t)$ is the mutual Euclidean distance $\delta_{i,j,t}$ between seed vertex v_i and seed vertex v_j over time and $\sigma_{i,j}$ is its standard deviation. $S = \frac{1}{N^2}\sum_{i,j}(\sigma_{i,j} + \sqrt{\rho_{i,j}})$ is a scaling term controlling the convergence behavior. We construct the entries of A such that the affinity values of vertex pairs with large average mutual distance is reduced, which forces our spectral clustering algorithm to put spatially far apart groups of vertices with similar motion into separate clusters.

Spectral clustering is our method of choice as it can robustly infer complex cluster topologies as they are typical for our motion segmentation problem. Instead of grouping the vertices directly based on the individual values $A_{i,j}$, spectral clustering proceeds by rearranging the l input samples in k well-separated clusters on the surface of a k-dimensional hypersphere. It achieves this by building a diagonal matrix D whose (i,i)-element is the sum of A's i-th row. Now the Laplacian matrix $L = D^{-1/2}A\ D^{-1/2}$ is built, its k largest eigenvalues $e_1, \ldots, e_k$ are computed and stacked into columns to form the matrix $X \in \mathbb{R}^{l \times k}$. The rows of X are normalized and considered as points in $\mathbb{R}^k$. Then the l row vectors are split into k clusters using standard k-means clustering. Every original sample vertex v_i is assigned to a cluster j if and only if row i of X was assigned to cluster j. We remind that k-means clustering is effective here because in the transformed data X clusters are well-separated.

Spectral clustering makes the clustering more robust against outliers and leads to a more robust and kinematically more meaningful segmentation than, for instance, standard k-means [7]. As an additional benefit, the optimal number of clusters k can be automatically calculated based on the data set's eigen-gap. In our system, we

Fig. 14.4 While with $k = 13$ patches (**left**) merely the larger rigid segments are identified, but the feet are merged with the lower legs, at $k = 31$ (**right**) the full kinematic detail has been discovered. Reprinted from [15] © Eurographics Association.

automatically cluster the seeds into k groups such that around 99.0% of the total variation of the data is explained. However, for some applications, as the system in Chapter 15, the automatic optimal segmentation is not always the best one. In this case, spectral clustering also allows the specification of a number of rigid surface patches to be used to segment the model. Fig. 14.4 shows the segmentation of the camel's mesh for two different values of k. At a smaller k-value, the lower legs and the hoofs form one cluster since the relative motion between these two was less significant than the relative motion between other segments. For a larger k-value, they have been split in two, which shows that with increasing level k of detail, our segmentation intuitively produces plausible and more detailed segmentations.

Using the k optimal vertex clusters, we create triangle clusters $T_0 \ldots T_{k-1} = T_{tri}$ by assigning each triangle $\Delta = (w_0, w_1, w_2) \in T_{tri}$ to the closest seed vertex class considering the average Euclidean distance from a seed vertex v_u to w_0, w_1, and w_2. The resulting clusters divide the mesh into k approximately rigid surface patches, Fig 14.3(right). Note that although a structurally motivated distance measure like the geodesic distance could also be used for clustering the triangles and to determine affinities in Eq. 14.1, our experiments show that similar results can be achieved using simple Euclidean distance which reduces the algorithm's computation time considerably. As seen in Sect. 14.6, our segmentation approach is able to create triangle patches that divide the mesh into plausible approximately rigid body parts.

14.3 Automatic Skeleton Extraction

Given the list of body segments, their associated seed vertices and triangle patches, we extract the kinematic skeleton structure of the animated mesh by first finding its kinematic topology (i.e. find which body parts are adjacent) and, thereafter, by estimating the positions of the interconnecting joints for the whole sequence.

To determine which body segments are adjacent, we analyze the triangles at the boundaries of the triangle patches. Body parts A and B are adjacent if they have mutually adjacent triangles in their respective patch boundaries. Unfortunately, in practice a patch may be adjacent to more than one other patch. If more than two patches are directly connected (e.g. head, torso and arm), we need to decide which segments are truly kinematically connected and which are not. Here we take a heuristic approach and consider only those patches to be adjacent that share the longest common boundary (in terms of the number of adjacent boundary triangles). For instance, if head, arm and torso are connected, we calculate the number of neighboring triangles for all combinations of patch pairings (e.g. head-torso, head-arm and torso-arm) and do not assign the pair head-arm as an adjacent segment since it has less neighbors in comparison with the other two options. For any adjacent pair of patches, a joint has to be found later. Note that in our system we assume that the body part in the center of gravity of the mesh at the reference time step is the root of the hierarchy.

In order to estimate the joint positions between two adjacent body segments A and B quickly, we only consider the information from the sets of seed vertices V_A and V_B located on these segments, and not the information from all vertices of $\mathcal{M}_{tri}$. Instead of solving for the complete sequence of joint positions, we significantly reduce the problem's complexity by first aligning the segment poses to a reference time step tr (usually $tr = 0$), then solving for a single optimal joint position at c_{tr} in the reference pose, and finally retransforming c_{tr} into the original poses of A and B.

To serve this purpose, for each time step t, we first compute two rigid body transforms $T_{A_{t \to tr}}$ and $T_{B_{t \to tr}}$ that align the positions of the seed vertices in both sets with the positions of the seed vertices V_A at the reference time step [8].

For finding c_{tr}, we follow an idea proposed in [12] and assume that a good estimate for the correct sequence of joint positions is the sequence of locations that minimizes the variance in joint-to-vertex distance for all seed vertices of the adjacent parts at all frames. Using this assumption, [1] solves for the joint location at the reference time c_{tr} by using a distance penalty based on the average Euclidean distance to regularize the solution. Alternatively, we use the regularization term proposed by [4], which makes the estimated joint position come closer to the centroid position b_t of the boundary curve between the two adjacent body parts at all time steps t. Therefore, we solve for c_{tr} by minimizing:

$$J(c_{tr}) = \frac{1}{2} * \sum_{v_a \in V_A} \sigma_a(c_{tr}) + \frac{1}{2} * \sum_{v_b \in V_B} \sigma_b(c_{tr}) + \alpha * d(c_{tr}, b_{tr}), \qquad (14.2)$$

where $\sigma_a(c_{tr})$ and $\sigma_b(c_{tr})$ corresponds to the Euclidean distance variance over time between the joint position c_{tr} and the vertex v_a and between c_{tr} and v_b, respectively. $d(c_{tr}, b_{tr})$ is the Euclidean distance between c_{tr} and b_{tr} at the reference time step. The coefficient α is used to regularize the solution, making the joint position be located as closed as possible to the interior of the mesh. The results in Sect. 14.6 were generated using a value of $\alpha = 0.05$ (which we found to be satisfactory in our experiments).

After solving Eq. 14.2 and finding the optimal joint location c_{tr}, the joint positions at all other frames can be easily computed by $c_t = T_{A_{t \to tr}}^{-1} * c_{tr}$. By applying the above procedure to all adjacent body parts, we reconstruct all joint positions for the whole sequence (see Fig. 14.5).

14.4 Motion Parameters Estimation

A consistent parameterization of the skeletal motion in terms of rotational joint parameters is only feasible in case the skeleton structure preserves constant dimensions over time. However, due to possible errors generated by aligning the body parts in the reference frame (mostly caused by subtle (non-rigid) relative motion between vertices on the same segment), the lengths of the bones in the skeleton may slightly vary over time. We enforce the bone lengths to be constant by stepping through the hierarchy of the estimated skeleton from the root down to the leaves and correcting the joint positions for each pair of subsequent joints in the kinematic chain separately such that the bone length constraint is satisfied.

Let c_t^i be the position of a joint i and c_t^{i-1} the position of its parent joint at time t. We are able to calculate the optimal value for the length of the bone connecting joint $i-1$ and i, $l_{i-1,i}$, over time and the new positions for the joints i, nc_t^i, by minimizing the following energy:

$$S(nc^i, l_{i-1,i}) = \sum_{t=0}^{N} \|c_t^i - nc_t^i\|^2 + (\|nc_t^i - c_t^{i-1}\| - l_{i-1,i})^2. \qquad (14.3)$$

The first term in Eq. 14.3 keeps the new joint position nc_t^i as close as possible to the old position, while the second term constrains the bone length to be the same in all frames.

After solving this equation for each pair of subsequent joints in the hierarchy, we obtain a consistent kinematic structure of the mesh $\mathcal{M}_{tri}$. To infer joint motion parameters, i.e. a rotational transformation R_t^i for all joints i at all times t, we first specify the skeletal pose at the first time step as reference pose (this is the best we can do given no explicit reference). Thereafter, we apply a Cyclic-Coordinate-Descent (CCD) like algorithm [14, 5] to infer all R_t^i relative to the reference using Euler angle parameterization. To this end, we optimize one joint variable at a time by calculating the positional error with respect to the estimated joint positions found for that time step. Since we have all in-between joint positions of each kinematic sub-chain, our method converges quickly and reliably. Finally, the translation of the root is stored as additional parameter for each frame.

14.5 Skinning Weight Computation

Skinning is the process of attaching the skeleton to the surface in such a way that changes in skeletal pose lead to plausible surface deformations. Although more advanced deformation schemes exist (see Sect. 13.1), we decided to use the standard linear blend skinning method [13], also called skeletal subspace deformation method - SSD, since it is widely supported in games and animation packages.

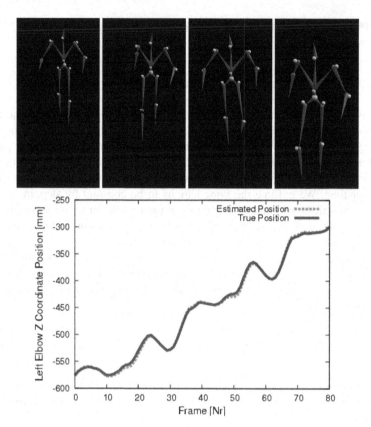

Fig. 14.5 (top) Visual comparison between the reconstructed joint positions and the true positions (shown as white spheres) at four different frames. **(bottom)** Plot of the low difference in z-coordinate between the reconstructed left elbow joint position and the ground truth position over time (biped walking sequence). Reprinted from [2] © Wiley-Blackwell.

Let $p_0(v_i)$ be the position of the vertex v_i of $\mathcal{M}_{tri}$ in the reference pose (or rest pose), let R_t^b be the transformation of the bone b from the reference to time t, and let $w^b(v_i)$ be the weight of the bone b for the vertex v_i. Note that the bone transformation R_t^b equals the transformation R_t^j of the preceding joint j from the hierarchy. SSD expresses the new position of vertex v_i at time t as $p_t(v_i) = \sum_b w_i^b R_t^b p_0(v_i)$. Therefore, in order to use the SSD method to re-animate the sequences using a more compact representation, we need to determine the bone weights w_i^b for each vertex v_i, i.e. we need to know how much each bone influences each vertex.

We employ the method proposed in [6] to determine the skinning weight distribution for each bone. This method computes the distribution based on the results of a heat diffusion process rather than based on simple vertex proximity to the bone, which makes the estimation process more robust. In contrast to their work, however, we consider the entire sequence of mesh and skeleton poses from the input when finding optimal weights. In particular, we first solve for the weight distributions w_f^b of each frame f separately, and thereafter average them to obtain the final distributions w^b.

When computing the weight distribution w_f^b we regard the volume of the model $\mathcal{M}_{tri}$ as an insulated heat-conducting body and force the temperature of the bone b to be 1 and the temperature of all others to be 0. The weight $w_f^b(v_i)$ equals the equilibrium temperature at v_i. For computational simplicity, the equilibrium equation is only solved on the mesh's surface yielding $\frac{\partial w_f^b}{\partial t} = \Delta w_f^b + H_f(p_f^b - w_f^b) = 0$. In our discrete case this can be reformulated as

$$(-\Delta_f + H_f)w_f^b = H_f p_f^b. \tag{14.4}$$

In this equation, Δ_f is the discrete Laplacian operator at frame f (see Sect 3), p_f^b is a vector where $p_f^b(v_i)$ equals 1 in case b is the nearest bone to vertex v_i and 0 otherwise. H_f is a diagonal matrix with entries $H_{ii} = 1/dist(v_i)^2$ representing the heat contribution weight of the nearest bone to vertex v_i at frame f. Here, $dist(v_i)$ is the Euclidean distance between vertex v_i and the nearest bone in case it is contained in the model's volume and 0 otherwise. The final weight distributions w^b for each bone is the average of the weights w_f^b for all frames.

The heat diffusion solution provides smooth and realistic blending weight distributions since it respects geodesic surface proximity during weight assignment rather than error-prone Euclidean proximity [6]. Furthermore, our experiments show that by computing the optimal weights from all available poses, our resulting skeletal animation reproduces the entire original mesh animation more faithfully, Sect. 14.6.

14.6 Results and Discussion

To demonstrate and validate our algorithm, we applied it to a set of mesh animations generated in a variety of different ways, see Table 14.1 for a list. Some synthetic sequences, such as the horse sequence (Fig. 14.1), were generated with a mesh deformation method [17]. Other synthetic sequences like the bird and the walking biped were originally created with a skeleton-based method which conveniently gives us ground truth data. We also have captured performances of humans at our disposition. The dancing and capoeira sequences, Fig. 14.7 and Fig. 14.9, were reconstructed by the performance capture approach described in Chapter 11. The cartwheel and posing sequences (Fig. 14.9) were obtained by using raw motion capture marker trajectories as constraints in our mesh-based animation framework described in Chapter 7.

Fig. 14.9 shows one original input mesh, the color-coded skinning weight distributions, and some poses of the original animation re-rendered using our skeleton-based reparametrization. A visual comparison between our result and the input, Fig. 14.7, shows that our result is visually almost indistinguishable from the original mesh animation and exhibits very natural surface deformations. Furthermore, visual inspection already suggests that the estimated kinematic structures are nicely

Fig. 14.6 Visual comparison between pre-defined skeleton embedded to the mesh **(left sub-images)** and the skeleton extracted by our approach **(right sub-images)**. Despite slight differences in the torso area, our estimated skeleton closely resembles the fitted template. Reprinted from [2] © Wiley-Blackwell.

embedded into the subjects at all frames and possess biologically plausible dimensions and hierarchies. Here, we would like to note again that all these results were obtained fully-automatically. Our new representation is very compact. For the horse animation, for instance, we only need to store geometry and skinning weights once, and for each time step only store 60 motion parameters (3-DOF per joint) rather than approximately 25000 coordinate values.

To get a quantitative impression of the faithfulness and quality of our results, we analyze individual aspects of our method more closely.

Skeleton Reconstruction

Since for most synthetic data we know the true sequence of joint positions, we are able to provide a quantitative estimate of the accuracy of our skeleton extraction and motion capture approach. Fig. 14.5(top) shows a visual comparison between the joint positions estimated by our approach and the true joint positions, shown as

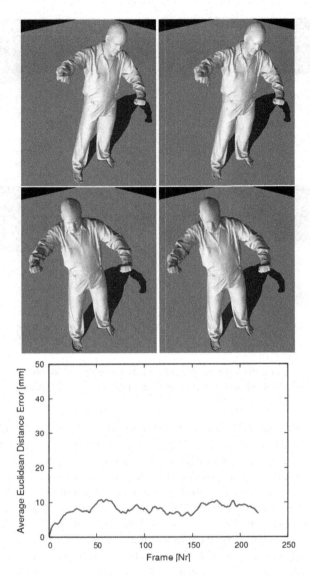

Fig. 14.7 (top-middle) Two pairs of images comparing the input (**left sub-images**) to our skeleton-based result (**right sub-images**). In either case the renderings are visually almost indistinguishable. (**bottom**) Plot showing the low average Euclidean distance error between input and reconstructed vertex positions for the human-sized model. Reprinted from [2] © Wiley-Blackwell.

white spheres, for the walking biped sequence. Fig. 14.5(bottom) illustrates the accuracy of the reconstructed motion parameters over time. The plot shows a comparison between the z-coordinate of the true and estimated positions of the left elbow joint for the same walking sequence. The difference between true and estimated joint

Fig. 14.8 New poses for the input mesh can be easily generated by simply changing the joint parameters of the extracted skeleton. Reprinted from [2] © Wiley-Blackwell.

positions is very small and consistent over time, which illustrates the robustness of our method. Similar low errors could be observed in all our sequences with available ground truth. The column JACC in Table 14.1 shows the average Euclidean distance error between estimated joint position and true joint position for all joints over time. Due to the lack of absolute coordinates, the error is given in percent of the longest bounding box dimension of the model. In all our examples, major misalignments between the original and the reconstructed skeleton could only be found if the part of the input corresponding to that joint was not prominently articulated.

Our automatically computed bone hierarchies closely match the skeletons that would typically be created by animators. This is demonstrated in Fig. 14.6, where we show a side-by-side comparison between our result and the skeleton fitted by the method of Baran et al. [6]. Although the topology of the root/spine area slightly differs, our calculated skeleton closely resembles the a priori fitted template.

Accuracy of reparameterized animation

Fig. 14.7(top) shows a comparison between two frames of the input dancing sequence (left sub-images) and the generated skeleton-based animation (right sub-images). Visually, almost no difference can be seen. Fig. 14.7(bottom) plots the consistently low average difference between the vertex positions of the input and

Table 14.1 Given an animated mesh sequence with T triangles (Δ) and N frames (FR), the processing times for segmenting the mesh into triangle patches (SEGM), to extract its kinematic structure and reconstruct its motion parameters (SKEL), and to calculate the skinning weights based on the input data (SKIN) are shown. Also, the low average difference between estimated joint positions and true joint locations (JACC) - in percent of the maximal side length of the overall bounding box - and the average difference between original and reconstructed vertex positions (ACCU) are indicated. Reprinted from [2] © Wiley-Blackwell.

SEQUENCE	FR	Δ	SEGM	SKEL	SKIN	JACC	ACCU
Horse	47	17K	4s	17s	7s/frame	N/A	0.56%
Bird	60	55K	5s	49s	10s/frame	2.9%	0.42%
Biped	80	32K	5s	36s	14s/frame	1.7%	0.52%
Cartwheel	120	7K	4s	63s	3s/frame	N/A	0.81%
Posing	280	7K	9s	261s	4s/frame	N/A	0.43%
Capoeira	150	106K	44s	244s	28s/frame	N/A	0.47%
Dancing	220	106K	37s	312s	28s/frame	N/A	0.37%

the reparameterized output over time for the dancing sequence. For the human-sized figure, the error is mostly below one centimeter which shows the high reconstruction quality also quantitatively. Column ACCU of Table 14.1 shows that similarly low errors are observed in the other test sequences.

Pose and animation editing

Using our system, we are able not only to recreate the original input based on a more compact representation, but can straightforwardly produce novel postures of the input mesh, Fig. 14.8. To this end, we only need to modify the joint parameters which can easily be done in any standard animation package. Since we have a complete set of motion parameters for the input, we can also easily modify aspects of the original animation by altering the joint parameter curves of selected joints.

Computation time

Table 14.1 lists the run times of each processing step in our algorithm. The second and third columns show the number of frames in each sequence (FR) and the number of triangles in each model (Δ). The column SEGM lists the time needed for clustering and mesh segmentation. Column SKEL lists the time needed to build the skeleton and estimate all motion parameters, and column SKIN lists the time needed to find the blending weights. With the exception of SKIN which shows per-frame times, all times given are for processing entire sequences. All run times were measured on an unoptimized single-threaded code running at a Laptop featuring an Intel Core Duo CPU with 1.7 GHz.

Fig. 14.9 Results obtained with different captured performances (top to bottom in each column): One frame of the input sequence, color-coded blending weight distribution, and two poses of the input recreated with our skeleton-based representation. Our method efficiently and fully-automatically converts mesh animations, created by animators or captured from moving subjects, into skeleton-based animations. Reprinted from [2] © Wiley-Blackwell.

Discussion

Our approach is subject to a few limitations. During skeleton extraction, it is impossible to locate a joint if there is no relative motion between adjacent body parts.

Therefore, in some of our sequences hands and feet are missed due to insignificant relative motion. However, we consider this to be a principal problem of any data-driven skeleton extraction method, and user interaction is feasible in this case.

Most remaining reconstruction inaccuracies are due to non-rigid deformation components in the input that are not well explainable by a rigid skeleton and linear skinning weights. However, alternative skinning methods can be applied to even further reduce the residual errors, e.g. [15, 10, 3, 19]. Furthermore, skeletal reparametrization works very well for subjects whose motion is largely due to a skeleton such as humans and most animals. In largely non-rigidly moving animations, such as a deforming piece of cloth, our algorithm would still determine a skeleton, but it is not physically plausible. Therefore, mesh-based editing approaches might be preferred in this case [11, 20].

Despite these limitations, in this chapter we have presented a fully-automatic method to extract a kinematic skeleton, joint motion parameters, and surface skinning weights from arbitrary mesh animations. The result is a compact representation of the original input that can be easily rendered and modified in standard skeleton-based animation tools without having to modify them. This way, we are able to preserve the great modeling flexibility of purely mesh-based approaches while making the resulting skeleton-less animations straightforwardly available to the animator's repertoire of processing tools.

Our results show that the efficient combination of skeleton learning and temporally-coherent blending weight computation enables us to effectively bridge the gap between the mesh-based and the skeleton-based animation paradigms.

References

1. de Aguiar, E., Theobalt, C., Seidel, H.-P.: Automatic learning of articulated skeletons from 3D marker trajectories. In: Bebis, G., Boyle, R., Parvin, B., Koracin, D., Remagnino, P., Nefian, A., Meenakshisundaram, G., Pascucci, V., Zara, J., Molineros, J., Theisel, H., Malzbender, T. (eds.) ISVC 2006. LNCS, vol. 4291, pp. 485–494. Springer, Heidelberg (2006)
2. de Aguiar, E., Theobalt, C., Thrun, S., Seidel, H.P.: Automatic conversion of mesh animations into skeleton-based animations. Computer Graphics Forum (Proc. Eurographics EG 2008) 27(2), 389–397 (2008)
3. Angelidis, A., Singh, K.: Kinodynamic skinning using volume-preserving deformations. In: SCA, pp. 129–140 (2007)
4. Anguelov, D., Koller, D., Pang, H., Srinivasan, P., Thrun, S.: Recovering articulated object models from 3d range data. In: Proc. of UAI, pp. 18–26 (2004)
5. Badler, N.I., Manoochehri, K.H., Baraff, D.: Multi-dimensional input techniques and articulated figure positioning by multiple constraints. In: SI3D, pp. 151–169 (1987)
6. Baran, I., Popović, J.: Automatic rigging and animation of 3d characters. ACM Trans. Graph. 26(3), 72 (2007)
7. Duda, R.O., Hart, P.E.: Pattern Classification, 2nd edn. Wiley, Chichester (2001)
8. Horn, B.K.P.: Closed-form solution of absolute orientation using unit quaternions. Journal of the Optical Society of America 4(4), 629–642 (1987)
9. James, D., Twigg, C.: Skinning mesh animations. ACM Transactions on Graphics (Proc. SIGGRAPH) 24(3) (2005)

10. Kavan, L., Collins, S., Zara, J., O'Sullivan, C.: Skinning with dual quaternions. In: ACM SIGGRAPH Symposium on Interactive 3D Graphics and Games, pp. 39–46 (2007)
11. Kircher, S., Garland, M.: Editing arbitrarily deforming surface animations. In: SIGGRAPH 2006, pp. 1098–1107 (2006)
12. Kirk, A.G., O'Brien, J.F., Forsyth, D.A.: Skeletal parameter estimation from optical motion capture data. In: CVPR, pp. 782–788 (2005)
13. Lewis, J.P., Cordner, M., Fong, N.: Pose space deformation: a unified approach to shape interpolation and skeleton-driven deformation. In: Proc. of ACM SIGGRAPH 2000, pp. 165–172 (2000)
14. Luenberger, D.G.: Introduction to Linear and Nonlinear Programming. New York (1973)
15. Merry, B., Marais, P., Gain, J.: Animation space: A truly linear framework for character animation. ACM Trans. Graph. 25(4), 1400–1423 (2006)
16. Ng, A.Y., Jordan, M., Weiss, Y.: On spectral clustering: Analysis and an algorithm. In: Proc. NIPS, pp. 849–856 (2002)
17. Sumner, R.W., Popović, J.: Deformation transfer for triangle meshes. In: Proc. ACM SIGGRAPH, pp. 399–405 (2004)
18. Theobalt, C., Rössl, C., de Aguiar, E., Seidel, H.P.: Animation collage. In: SCA 2007, pp. 271–280 (2007)
19. Wang, R.Y., Pulli, K., Popović, J.: Real-time enveloping with rotational regression. ACM Trans. Graph. 26(3), 73 (2007)
20. Xu, W., Zhou, K., Yu, Y., Tan, Q., Peng, Q., Guo, B.: Gradient domain editing of deforming mesh sequences. ACM TOG 26(3), 84 (2007)
21. Yamauchi, H., Gumhold, S., Zayer, R., Seidel, H.P.: Mesh segmentation driven by gaussian curvature. Visual Computer 21(8-10), 649–658 (2005)

Chapter 15
Designing Non-photorealistic Animation Collages

In this chapter, we present a method to automatically transform mesh animations into animation collages, i.e. a new non-photorealistic rendering style for animations. By automatically decomposing input animations and fitting a shape from the database into each segment, our algorithm creates a new rendering style. It has many applications in arts, non-photorealistic rendering, and animated movie productions.

An animation collage is a complete reassembly of the original animation in a new abstract visual style that imitates the spatio-temporal shape and deformation of the input. Many researchers in computer graphics have been inspired by the idea to develop algorithms that enable the computer and even unexperienced users to reproduce the look of certain styles of visual arts, such as collages. Kim et al. [10] develop a system that can automatically turn arbitrary photographs into collage mosaics that comprise of an arrangement of elementary image tiles. Rother et al. [14] automatically arrange and blend photographs from a database into a perceptually pleasing way. Gal et al. [5] show results of a method to approximate static 3D shapes with other meshes, but they do not handle the general case of mesh animations.

In contrast, this chapter presents a method allowing a computer artist to automatically convert his/her favorite mesh animation into a moving assembly of 3D shape primitives in a database. This so-called animation collage is glued together in such a way that it approximates the sequence of shapes from the original mesh animation, while deforming in the same spatio-temporally consistent way as the original. While our method can fully-automatically build moving collages, it also purposefully gives the artist the possibility to post-process and fine-tune the results according to his/her imagination.

An overview of our system is presented in Sect. 15.1. It first automatically decomposes the input mesh animation into moving approximately rigid volume segments, henceforth called *animation cells*, Sect. 15.2 and Sect. 15.3. This decomposition is learned from the moving input meshes by means of a spectral clustering approach, Sect 14.2. Thereafter, it employs a spatio-temporal matching criterion that

E. de Aguiar: Animation & Performance Capture Using Digi. Models, COSMOS 5, pp. 149–162.
springerlink.com © Springer-Verlag Berlin Heidelberg 2010

analyzes the motion and deformation of each animation cell and finds a shape primitive in the database that best approximates its time-varying geometry, Sect. 15.4. Shape primitives and cells are spatio-temporally aligned, and the fitted shapes are moved and deformed according to the deformation of the cells, Sect 15.5. Since it is also our goal to develop new algorithmic recipes for a novel artistic tool, an animator can influence the final result at all stages of the processing pipeline, Sect 15.6.

The main contribution of this chapter is a system [15] to

- automatically transform mesh animations, which are created directly by animators or captured using our previous performance capture methods, into animation collages.

Our software prototype is easy to use and allows even untrained users to create very aesthetic collages. Therefore, our system is an interesting add-on to the graphics artist's toolbox, with many applications in visual arts, non-photorealistic rendering, and productions of games and cartoons.

15.1 Overview

As in Chapter 14, the input to our algorithm is an animated mesh sequence comprising of N frames, represented by a mesh model $\mathcal{M}_{tri} = (V_{tri}, T_{tri})$ and position data $p_t(v_j) = (x_j, y_j, z_j)_t$ for each vertex $v_j \in V_{tri}$ at all time steps t. The coordinate sets $P_t = \{p_t(v_j)\}$ together with $\mathcal{M}_{tri}$ describe a time-varying surface. The second input element is a database of K static shapes, each being represented as a textured triangle mesh.

The first step in our pipeline is the motion-decomposition of the mesh. To this end, we employ the method described in Sect. 14.2 that analyzes the motion of the mesh and delivers contingent triangle patches representing approximately rigid elements, as shown in Fig. 15.1(a). To enable the fitting of shape primitives, we transform the rigid surface elements into approximately rigid volume cells, so-called *animation cells*. To this end, a sequence of medial axis meshes is computed from the animation which, in conjunction with the previously identified rigid surface segments, is used to create these closed volume cells, Sect. 15.3 and Figs. 15.1(b),(c). Once the animation cells have been identified, we automatically fit to each of them a shape primitive from the database, Sect. 15.4. The final moving collages are generated by deforming the fitted shapes according to the transformation of their respective animation cells, Fig. 15.1(d). To achieve this, we generate spatio-temporally consistent offset meshes from the animation cells that drive the shape primitives' deformations, Sect. 15.5.

15.2 Rigid Body Segmentation

The first step in our pipeline segments the input animation given by $\mathcal{M}_{tri}$ and P_t into spatially coherent triangle patches that undergo approximately the same rigid transformations over time. Our motivation for decomposing the mesh into approximately

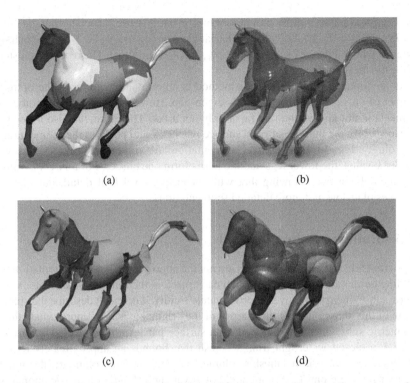

Fig. 15.1 Important steps in our pipeline: the mesh is decomposed into rigidly moving surface patches (**a**), skeletons are extracted (**b**), and animation cells assembled (**c**), here only some cells are shown. Shapes are spatio-temporally fitted to the cells and deformed over time to build the animation collage (**d**). Reprinted from [15] © Eurographics Association.

rigid patches is that this seems intuitive and plausible to the viewer. Many characters in cartoons and animation films, for instance the main actors in 20-th century Fox's "Robots" [13], were rendered in this particular style.

The deformations of general mesh animations can not be described by rigid transformations alone. Animators often purposefully combine rigid transformations with non-rigid ones in order to create a lifelike look. In contrast to motion segmentation approaches that generate merely a statistically plausible segmentation, we intend to isolate the underlying rigid deformations from the non-rigid ones in a kinematically plausible way. By this, we mean that in case there exists a true kinematic segment hierarchy, our method approximates it as good as possible. For us, it is also important that regions on the surface are spatially connected. Only if this is assured, a faithful decomposition into volume cells becomes feasible, Sect. 15.3.

We apply the motion-driven segmentation method described in Sect. 14.2 to divide the input animation into rigidly moving coherent triangle patches as shown in Fig. 14.4. The approach is initialized by first selecting l sample vertices distributed evenly on the model. The motion trajectories of these vertices throughout the whole animation form the input to our spectral clustering approach which groups them into k approximately rigidly moving groups. From this, we associate triangle clusters $T_0 \ldots T_{k-1} = T_{tri}$ by assigning each triangle $\Delta = (w_0, w_1, w_2) \in T_{tri}$ to the marker vertex v_j whose average distance to w_0, w_1, and w_2 is minimal. The resulting clusters divide the mesh in k segments.

As mentioned in Sect. 14.2, our method is able to automatic infer the optimal number of clusters from the dataset's eigen-gap. However, the optimal number of segments is not always the one favored by an artist. Therefore, we also allow the user to specify the number of rigid surface patches k and perform the segmentation accordingly. Fig. 14.4 shows two segmentations for the camel's model. Using a smaller k-value, the lower legs and the hoofs form one cluster. For a larger k-value, they are split in two, showing that with increasing level k of detail, our method produces plausible and more detailed segmentations.

15.3 Building Animation Cells

Approximately rigid surface patches are not the appropriate shape representation for building animation collages. Although each patch is the outer boundary of a volumetric subsegment that moves approximately rigidly, it does not describe the spatial extent of this subsegment in the interior of the original mesh. To approximate these volumetric subsegments, we extend each surface patch into a so-called *animation cell*, i.e. a closed watertight triangle mesh that bounds an approximately rigidly moving slice of the original mesh's volume, Fig. 15.1(c). This volumetric decomposition of input animations has a couple of advantages. First, volumetric animation cells define 3D placeholders to which approximating shapes are to be fitted in order to generate visually pleasing collages with decent shape and deformation approximation. Thus, volumetric decomposition is a clever way to break down the fitting problem for the whole mesh into a set of fitting problems for individual cells. Furthermore, by deforming approximating shapes like their encompassing rigid cells, the deformation of the shapes remains in visually pleasing bounds.

The input for building animation cells is the set of rigid surface patches $T_0, \ldots, T_{k-1}$ that was computed in the previous section. It is our goal to extend each surface patch into a closed and watertight animation cell mesh. Looking only at the graph structure of each patch, this is easily achieved by inserting a new vertex for every boundary loop, triangulating the arising fan, and thereby removing the boundary loop. Although the principal idea is fairly easy, a proper way to insert the additional vertex for the boundary loop is crucial.

We firstly compute a sequence of medial axis meshes $S_0, \ldots, S_{N-1}$ from the input animation, Fig. 15.1(b). The number of vertices and the connectivity of each S_i matches the properties of the respective $\mathcal{M}^i_{tri}$ that it was computed from: for computing the skeletal mesh S_i, we employ the Voronoi-based two-sided approximation of the medial axis that has originally been proposed in [7]. Every vertex of $\mathcal{M}^i_{tri}$ is associated with a Voronoi cell. One-to-one correspondences between the vertices of $\mathcal{M}^i_{tri}$ and the vertices of S_i are established by using the Voronoi poles as skeletal mesh vertices [1]. The connectivity of S_i is copied from $\mathcal{M}^i_{tri}$. In order to remove undesired spikes in the skeletal mesh, we employ tangential Laplacian smoothing.

Fig. 15.2 An animation cell for the center segment of the horse (**left**), the strawberry fitted to it (**middle**), and the offset cell for the center segment (**right**), all shown for the same time step. Reprinted from [15] © Eurographics Association.

As the skeletons share the graph structure of the animation meshes, they can be partitioned into the same patches. In the following, we describe how to build animation cells for all patches at a single time step t. By applying the same procedure to all time steps, we generate the appropriately deformed versions of each cell. Consider a patch T_k and its associated vertex positions taken from P_t. For all boundary loops of T_k at a time step t, we compute the center of gravity of associated vertex positions in the skeleton S_t. The new vertex for fan-triangulation of the boundary loop is positioned at this center. Fig. 15.2 (left) illustrates this using a center segment of the horse animation as an example.

Note that a simple strategy like choosing the center of gravity of the boundary loop's vertices for fan-triangulation would not have fulfilled our requirements. Our experiments showed that, in this case, very flat animation cells may occur for extreme geometric configurations which would lead to inappropriate volumes for the subsequent steps of our method. Depending on the geometric setting, similar problems may occur if one tries to directly triangulate a hole without inserting a vertex. Although our cell decomposition does not strictly partition the volume, it generates volume slices that are tailored to our purpose.

15.4 Assembling the Collage

As already outlined in the previous section, the sequence of moving animation cells can be regarded as a sequence of volumetric placeholders to which approximating shapes from the database are fitted. While, by this means, it may not be possible to exactly reproduce the true shape of each cell, in particular its outer surface, the overall appearance of the mesh animation is still faithfully approximated. The decomposition of the animation into cells also bears many further algorithmic advantages since the overall fitting problem simplifies to a fitting problem between individual shapes and segments. Furthermore, it becomes easier to assure that the shapes to fit not only match the outlines of their respective animation cells at a single time step. Since the animation cells undergo mainly rigid deformations, the slight non-rigid deformations of the approximate shapes that may be necessary to assure good approximation over the whole sequence can be kept in reasonable bounds, Sect. 15.5.

To put this into practice, a shape similarity measure is needed (Sect. 15.4.1) that is applied in our spatio-temporal matching and alignment approach to fit a database shape to a deforming animation cell, as described in Sect. 15.4.2.

15.4.1   Shape Similarity Measure

Due to the diversity of database shapes, and potential differences in orientation and uniform scaling, we require a similarity measure that is rotation-, pose- and scale-independent. Spherical harmonic descriptors fulfill all these requirements and have proven to be superior to many other global descriptors [9]. Given a mesh K, we compute its spherical harmonic descriptor as follows: first, the spatial occupancy function $O(x,y,z)$ is sampled on a regular grid within the mesh's bounding box by rasterizing the mesh into a voxel volume of dimension $\ell_1 \times \ell_2 \times \ell_3$ [12, 11]. The voxel volume is intersected with q equidistant spheres $W_0, \ldots, W_{q-1}$ that are concentrically arranged around the center of gravity of the voxel set. The discretized occupancy function is resampled on the surface of each spherical shell, yielding q spherical functions $o_0(\theta, \phi), \ldots, o_{q-1}(\theta, \phi)$. Each of these q spherical functions is decomposed into its harmonic frequency components as

$$f_\ell(\theta, \phi) = \sum_{m=-\ell}^{m=\ell} a_{\ell m} Y_\ell^m(\theta, \phi),$$

where ℓ is the frequency band, $a_{\ell m}$ is the m-th coefficient on a band ℓ, and Y_ℓ^m is the m-th spherical harmonic basis function for a band ℓ [6]. For each spherical function, the norms of its frequency components are computed as

$$SH(o_h) = \{\|f_0(\theta, \phi)\|, \|f_1(\theta, \phi)\|, \ldots, \|f_{\ell-1}(\theta, \phi)\|\}.$$

The complete shape descriptor $D(K)$ is the two-dimensional $q \times h$-array that is indexed by the sphere radius and the frequency band. For our purpose, we found that descriptors with $h = 20$ and $\ell = 10$ are sufficient.

The difference $d(D_1, D_2)$ between two descriptors D_1 and D_2 is obtained by interpreting each of them as $(q \cdot h)$-dimensional vectors and computing the angle that they span.

15.4.2   Spatio-temporal Shape Fitting

Using the above shape descriptor and the associated distance measure, we find a shape from the database that best matches the time-varying shape of each animation cell throughout the whole sequence. To keep processing times and memory consumption in reasonable bounds while sampling the range of deformations sufficiently densely, we propose the following approach to fit a shape to one animation

Fig. 15.3 Effect of spatio-temporal fitting for the tail of the camel (**left**). One frame of the result animation is shown with a single (**center**) or three representative time steps (**right**) used during spatio-temporal fitting. Reprinted from [15] © Eurographics Association.

cell Z_j: at first, a set of representative time steps $0 \leq t_1, \ldots, t_r < N$ is chosen in which the whole mesh undergoes a characteristic range of deformations. Let the vertex positions of Z_j at the r time steps be $P_{t_1}(Z_j), \ldots, P_{t_r}(Z_j)$. For each of the r cell poses, a descriptor is computed, yielding a set $U = \{D_{t_1}(Z_j), \ldots, D_{t_r}(Z_j)\}$. For each of the shapes in the database and their associated descriptors D_i, a global distance to all descriptors in U is computed as

$$d_{\text{glob}}(D_i, U) = \sum_{t \in t_1, \ldots, t_r} d(D_i, D_t(Z_j)) \quad \text{for } 0 \leq i < K.$$

The above distance assesses the spatio-temporal goodness of fit between a database shape and a cell over time. Accordingly, the index c of the database shape that matches the shape of Z_j at all representative time steps best is found as

$$c = \underset{i}{\arg\min} \, d_{\text{glob}}(D_i, U).$$

Database shape c is fitted to the single pose $P_{t_m}(Z_j)$ of Z_j out of all the representative poses which best matches the shape of c, thus

$$t_m = \underset{t \in \{t_1, \ldots, t_r\}}{\arg\min} \, d_{\text{glob}}(D_c, P_t(Z_j)).$$

By this way, we guarantee that the shape is fitted to the optimally matching configuration of the cell, and thus the required transformation of c during the fitting itself is minimal. The effect of spatio-temporal fitting is compared to single time step fitting in Fig. 15.3.

The fitting itself first coarsely registers shape c and Z_j in pose $P_{t_m}(Z_j)$ by aligning their centers of gravities and principal components in orientation and scaling. Thereafter, the initial fitting is refined by running an ICP-like alignment [2].

Although shape matching and fitting are fully automatic processes, user interaction is possible to meet artistic preferences. On the one hand, a user can restrict matching to a subset of the database or even manually choose a collage shape which will be fitted into the cell. Additionally, a user can also manually adjust the fitted shape's position, scale and orientation.

Finally, we note that, while there are many applications for *partial* shape matching, the use of a *global* approach is essential to our method, as our goal is to faithfully fill in the whole cell. This way, self-intersections and artifacts during the animation are minimized since the cells have a near-rigid structure. Furthermore, bigger holes in the collage are prevented. Consequently, we decided to fit only one shape per cell to provide the most plausible results for the animation.

15.5 Animating the 3D Collage

In the final stage of our method, we compute the animation collage from the set of animation cells and associated collage shapes. Note that each of the collage shapes has potentially been fitted to a different reference time step t_m by the procedure described in the previous section.

Our approach proceeds again cell-wise; per-frame transformation of the animation cells is propagated to the fitted shapes. We consider this transformation as a general deformation of the cell, which is expected to be nearly rigid. Among the many surface deformation methods which are available in the literature, we chose free-form deformation based on 3D mean-value coordinates [3, 4, 8], because it can directly process our input data, produces good results, and is robust and simple in implementation. Using the standard approach, the triangulation of the animation cell would serve directly as control mesh for the deformation. The collage shape is rigidly fitted into the geometry of the animation cell $P_{t_m}(Z)$ at a reference time step t_m, and then mean value coordinates are used to reconstruct shapes which deform like the geometry of cell $P_t(Z)$ at any other time step $0 \leq t < N$. However, there are two requirements which render this immediate deformation impractical for our special animation collage setting: first, we want to provide the user some additional

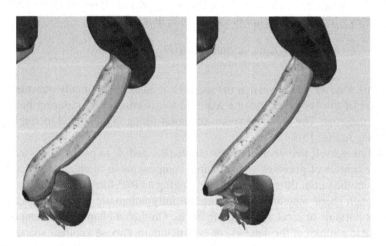

Fig. 15.4 With larger offset segments, the fruits in the horse's leg deform more stiffly (**right**) than with tighter offsets (**left**). Reprinted from [15] © Eurographics Association.

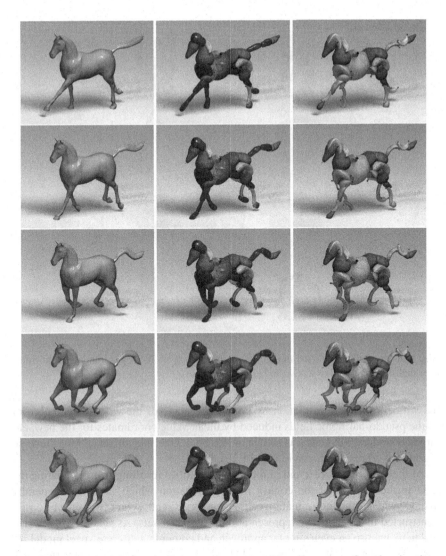

Fig. 15.5 Our method automatically generates moving 3D collages out of mesh animations by rebuilding them as moving assemblies of shape primitives. In the example above, the galloping horse (**first column**) has been transformed into two galloping sets of fruits (**second and third columns**). Reprinted from [15] © Eurographics Association.

global control over the deformation, and second, we have to ensure numerical robustness. Both requirements are related, and we apply a two-step deformation approach with spatio-temporal offsets.

The key idea of our deformation is to use certain morphological offsets of the animation cells as control meshes, i.e. the cells' geometry is extruded in the direction of the surface normal (but avoiding self-intersections). By this way, we can control

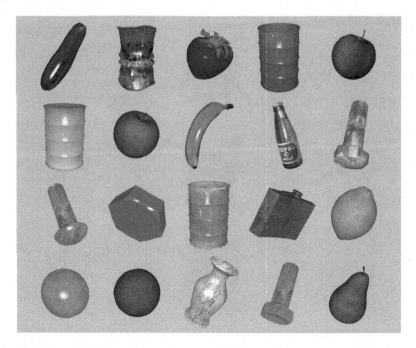

Fig. 15.6 Shape database used in our system comprising of 20 shapes, ranging from fruits, over industrial shapes like screws, to barrels and bottles.

the stiffness of the deformation by taking advantage of the well-known behavior of the pseudo-harmonic fields induced by mean value coordinates for the new, enlarged boundary polyhedra, as shown in Fig. 15.4. One such offset cell for the torso segment of a horse is shown in Fig. 15.2(right)

At the same time, we avoid numerical instabilities resulting from evaluating the field in the vicinity of the control mesh, a situation which cannot be generally avoided when using the animation cells' geometry directly. Our offsets can be easily constructed in a volumetric representation using level-sets. As accuracy is not crucial here, we use an even simpler approach and compute a discrete voxel model for each animation cell mesh following [11], which is then dilated and converted back into a triangle mesh using marching cubes. Here the voxel resolution and dilation radius define the offset radius. Then, we compute an offset cell for each animation cell with respect to the reference time step. The computation is efficient and guarantees watertightness and no self-intersections. However, we lose control over the combinatorial structure of the offset mesh, i.e. it does not share the animation cell's connectivity, and an alternative mapping to the animation cell need to be provided by the second deformation step.

The final animation of a single collage shape proceeds as follows. First, the time-dependent geometry of the animation cell is used as control mesh to compute a deformed offset cell. Second, the offset cell is used as control mesh and its deformation is propagated to the collage shape. Note that, by volumetric construction, the genus of the offset cell might differ from that of the respective animation cell. However, using the free-form deformation approach influencing the whole volume of the animation cell, this does not imply any problem. The offset radius provides an additional parameter to control the effect of the deformation: the more distant the offset, the stiffer the deformation. Fig. 15.4 shows that the shapes in the horse's leg bend more crisply, if the offset segments are tighter. While this parameter has no physically plausible meaning, we find it intuitive to use.

15.6   Results and Discussion

We have generated a variety of animation collages from mesh sequences of a galloping and a collapsing horse, a galloping camel, as well as two scanned humans performing a motion captured jump and a cartwheel. For none of the sequences, ground truth kinematics, e.g. in the form of animation skeletons, are available. Our shape database comprises of 20 collage shapes, ranging from fruits, over industrial shapes like screws, to barrels and bottles, Fig. 15.6. A variety of animation collages with different appealing visual styles were created, Fig. 15.8. The collages do not only have very aesthetic looks at a single time step, but nicely approximate the spatio-temporal appearance of the input animation, see Fig. 15.5 and, in particular, the resulting video.

The top row in Fig. 15.8 shows freeze-frames from the front and the back of an animation collage showing a jumping human. For the original sequence, motion capture data was used to animate a laser-scan using the method described in Chapter 7. With both fruits, as well as barrels, bottles, and screws, the 25 computed animation cells are both faithfully and sometimes funnily approximated. We particularly like the head being automatically approximated by a strawberry or a pear. Due to our offset-based deformation, the moving collages maintain the subtle motion details of the input which lends them a very human-like motion style.

The galloping horse is shown for fine and coarse segmentations with 35 and 17 animation cells in the upper middle row in Fig. 15.8. In comparison, one sees clearly

Fig. 15.7 Although the automatic result generated with our framework looks nice (**left**), the user is able to perform small changes at the tail and the leg of the animation collage to match personal preferences (**right**).

Table 15.1 Typical animation data. Shown are time steps N, number of triangles in the mesh Δ, and number of animation cells k. Furthermore, measured computation times (in seconds) are given for the four parts of the pipeline: Seg = Rigid patch segmentation; Cell = Animation cell + offset cell computation for each sequence; Fit = Shape fitting and alignment; Anim = Animation of the collage. Reprinted from [15] © Eurographics Association.

Seq.	N	Δ	k	Seg	Cell	Fit	Anim
jumping	216	26 312	25	416	401	46	171
gal. horse	48	16 843	35	297	190	64	134
camel	47	43 758	13	914	139	59	131
cartwheel	120	7 318	11	45	188	22	68

the non-rigid transformation for the coarse segmentations, for instance, in the lower legs where the hoofs are not covered by additional cells. However, even these deformations appear rather natural due to stiffness provided by the offset cells. Of course the individual impression depends on the viewers particular expectations and preferences, and spending more animation cells usually leads to better approximations of rigid parts. Moreover, our choice of using a single collage shape per cell is justified by the fact that the animation looks plausible, and there are few holes and self-intersections.

The galloping camel is shown for fine (lower middle row) and coarse segmentations (bottom row) with 31 and 13 animation cells in Fig. 15.8, respectively. We would like to point out the nice approximation of the hunch, e.g. by pears (coarse) and by bananas (fine). Specially, the arrangement of bananas is non-trivial, and the impression of a sophisticated design is given. Such arrangements are enabled by the partition in animation cells, and the example thus nicely confirms our algorithmic approach to break the fitting problem into cell-wise problems.

The majority of the results in Fig. 15.8 was generated fully-automatically. Only in some cases, marked with a black dot in the upper right, we changed the position or the kind of at most two shapes to match personal preferences, Fig. 15.7.

Table 15.1 summarizes information on input animation complexity and run times measured on a Pentium IV 3.0 GHz. Our approach is very efficient: run times are dominated by rigid body segmentation (Seg) and cell generation (Cell), both of which need to be run just once per input sequence. Shape fitting and alignment (Fit), as well as the animation of the collage (Anim), are performed once for each collage style created from an input sequence. Even for sequences with more than 200 frames, both steps can be finished in less than four minutes. Run times could be further sped up by working with decimated input or cell meshes, however, we always worked on the originals.

Our approach is subject to a couple of limitations. As mentioned in Sect. 14.6, while our clustering algorithm provides excellent results for the shown input animations, its output generally depends on these inputs: a meaningful segmentation can only be expected if there is actual relative motion of all limbs in an animation. We conclude that this approach works best for animations with kinematic structure. Inherently, fitting is limited by the shapes available in the database. If no proper shape

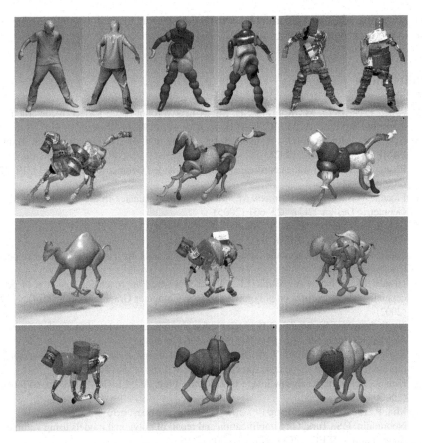

Fig. 15.8 Different visual styles for distinct frames of a jumping human, a galloping horse, and a galloping camel sequence. Black dots in the upper right mark animations including manual changes of position or kind of at most two shape primitives. Reprinted from [15] © Eurographics Association.

is available, unnatural deformations may be necessary. As the database also defines the visual style, we leave this as an artistic problem that has to be considered by the user. From a more technical point of view, our approach requires that segments span a volume. The approach is thus not able to fit collage shapes to nearly planar segments. Note that the spatio-temporal segmentation, which provides the segments, is not at all affected.

Furthermore, for fitting, we assume that the animation cells are in motion and hence being transformed. This is different from considering a static fitting problem, where alternative approaches such as Gal et al. [5] may show better results, and where it may be advantageous to allow for more shapes per cell.

Despite these limitations, we present a novel approach to fully-automatically generate animation collages from input mesh animations, providing a compendium of spatio-temporal matching and segmentation techniques. Our software prototype is an interesting add-on to the graphics artist's toolbox and also allows untrained people to produce high-quality results.

References

1. Amenta, N., Bern, M., Kamvysselis, M.: A new voronoi-based surface reconstruction algorithm. In: Proc. ACM SIGGRAPH, pp. 415–421 (1998)
2. Besl, P.J., McKay, N.D.: A method for registration of 3-d shapes. IEEE Trans. PAMI 14(2), 239–256 (1992)
3. Floater, M.S.: Mean value coordinates. Computer Aided Geometric Design 20(1), 19–27 (2003)
4. Floater, M.S., Kós, G., Reimers, M.: Mean value coordinates in 3D. Computer Aided Geometric Design 22(7), 623–631 (2005)
5. Gal, R., Sorkine, O., Popa, T., Sheffer, A., Cohen-Or, D.: 3d collage: Expressive non-realistic modeling. In: NPAR 2007, pp. 7–14 (2007)
6. Green, R.: Spherical harmonic lighting: The gritty details. In: Tutorial: Game Develpers Conference (2003)
7. Hisada, M., Belyaev, A., Kunii, T.L.: A skeleton-based approach for detection of perceptually salient features on polygonal surfaces. Computer Graphics Forum 21(4), 1–12 (2002)
8. Ju, T., Schaefer, S., Warren, J.D.: Mean value coordinates for closed triangular meshes. ACM TOG (Proc. SIGGRAPH) 24(3), 561–566 (2005)
9. Kazhdan, M., Funkhouser, T., Rusinkiewicz, S.: Rotation invariant spherical harmonic representation of 3d shape descriptors. In: Proc. SGP, pp. 156–164 (2003)
10. Kim, J., Pellacini, F.: Jigsaw image mosaics. In: Proc. ACM SIGGRAPH, pp. 657–664 (2002)
11. Min, P.: Binvox (2003), http://www.cs.princeton.edu/~min/binvox/
12. Nooruddin, F.S., Turk, G.: Simplification and repair of polygonal models using volumetric techniques. IEEE TVCG 9(2), 191–205 (2003)
13. Robots (2005), http://www.robotsmovie.com
14. Rother, C., Bordeaux, L., Hamadi, Y., Blake, A.: Autocollage. ACM Transactions on Graphics (Proc. SIGGRAPH) 25(3), 847–852 (2006)
15. Theobalt, C., Rössl, C., de Aguiar, E., Seidel, H.P.: Animation collage. In: SCA 2007, pp. 271–280 (2007)

Chapter 16
Conclusions

This book has presented novel algorithms to accurately capture, manipulate and realistically render real-world human performances, going beyond the limits of related capture techniques. Each method described in this work can be regarded as a specific solution to a challenging problem or as a building block that enables the development of novel applications. The methods outlined in this book have been originally tailored to deal with human actors. However, the fundamental principles are also applicable to a larger class of real-world scenes.

In part I of this book, we described how we model a real-world camera, and the kinematics, shape and appearance of a real-world subject in a computer. We also detailed the differential-based mesh deformation methods, which are used throughout the book to manipulate and track the input static scanned model. Furthermore, we presented the technical components of a new acquisition setup that provides high quality data for the different projects proposed in the book. Our studio allows us to generate realistic virtual doubles of real-world subjects by providing high-quality models and multiple video streams of the subject performing. The description of our studio also serves as a practical guide for people planning to build such facility.

Part II of this book introduced a simple framework to reduce the overhead caused by the traditional skeleton-based animation pipeline. By abandoning the concept of a kinematic skeleton, which most commercial softwares rely on, our mesh-based algorithms enable animators, or even untrained users, to quickly and effectively create realistic animations. The first approach (Chapter 6) and its extension (Chapter 7) integrate into the traditional animation workflow and simplify the whole procedure by employing mesh deformation methods to guide the motion generation and the motion transfer processes. Moreover, our experiments have shown that our new pipeline is able to simultaneous solve the animation, the surface deformation, and the motion retargeting problem.

Our proposed approach streamlines the whole pipeline from laser-scanning to animation from marker-based or marker-less motion capture data, and it is a step towards simplifying the traditional, not so straightforward acquisition-to-animation pipeline. As future work, we plan to incorporate a volumetric mesh deformation method, as the one presented in Sect. 3.3, to guide the motion transfer process. By

E. de Aguiar: Animation & Performance Capture Using Digi. Models, COSMOS 5, pp. 163–165.
springerlink.com   © Springer-Verlag Berlin Heidelberg 2010

this means, local cross-sectional areas are preserved, which will enable us to handle extreme deformations properly. We also would like to add intuitive key-framing capabilities into our framework.

In part III, we have described the evolution of a system to directly capture real-world performances using a high-quality deformable model and multi-view video sequences. We demonstrated that by explicitly abandoning any traditional skeletal or motion parameterization and by posing performance capture as deformation capture, acquisition methods with a high level of flexibility and versatility can be developed. As a result, a spatio-temporally coherent dynamic scene representation can be produced which can easily be modified by animators.

The first algorithm is described in Chapter 9. By combining an optical flow-based 3D correspondence estimation technique with a fast Laplacian-based tracking scheme, the method is able to accurately and automatically capture both pose and surface deformation of human actors wearing everyday apparel. The second algorithm is presented in Chapter 10. The purely passive hybrid tracking approach is able to identify and track the 3D trajectories of features on a moving subject without requiring any a priori information or optical markers. By combining the trajectories, a static laser-scanned model and an efficient deformation technique, the human scan can be animated and follows the same motion as its real-world counterpart.

In Chapter 11, we have presented our more advanced video-based performance capture system that augments the previously described approaches and overcomes many of their shortcomings. It produces a novel dense and feature-rich output format comprising of spatio-temporally coherent high-quality geometry, lifelike motion data, and surface texture of recorded actors. This is achieved by combining efficient volume- and surface-based deformation schemes, a multi-view analysis-through-synthesis procedure, and a multi-view stereo approach. By this means, our method is able to reconstruct an unprecedented range of real-world scenes at a high level of detail. It supplements and exceeds the capabilities of optical capturing systems that are widely used in the industry, and provides animators and CG artists with a new level of flexibility in acquiring and modifying real-world content.

By being completely passive, our performance capture methods also enable us to record the subject's appearance. By combining the input footage with our high-quality spatio-temporally coherent scene representation, a system to render high-quality 3D Videos can be created, which enables convincing renditions of the recorded subject from arbitrary synthetic viewpoints. This combination also opens the door for attacking new challenging reconstruction problems that were hard due to the lack of a decent dynamic scene capture technology.

Currently, there is a resolution limit to our capture techniques. Some of the high-frequency details, such as fine wrinkles in clothing or details of the face, has been part of the laser-scan in the first place. The deformation on this level of detail is not actually captured, but it is "baked in" to the deforming surface. In the future, we want to investigate ways to capture such complex time-varying details. We also intend to create tools for higher-level 3D Video editing operations.

In part IV of this book, we proposed novel algorithmic solutions for processing mesh animations, either generated by animators or acquired by our performance captured methods. With our proposed tools, we have made important contributions to the animator toolbox with a variety of applications in visual arts, movie and game productions.

The first approach is presented in Chapter 14 and enables the fully-automatic conversion of a mesh animation into a skeleton-based animation. Our results show that the efficient combination of skeleton learning and temporally-coherent blending weight computation enables us to effectively bridge the gap between the mesh-based and the skeleton-based animation paradigms. This way, we are able to preserve the great modeling flexibility of purely mesh-based approaches while making the resulting skeleton-less animations straightforwardly available to the animator's repertoire of processing tools.

The second method is presented in Chapter 15 and converts a mesh animation into a novel non-photorealistic animation style, the so-called animation collage. Our system is able to fully-automatically generate animation collages from input mesh animations, providing a compendium of spatio-temporal matching and segmentation techniques. Our software prototype is an interesting add-on to the graphics artist's toolbox and also allows untrained people to produce high-quality results.

The methods described in this book demonstrate that today it is possible to create, manipulate and render authentic virtual doubles of real-world actors performing. Although most projects are still research prototypes, we are convinced that the algorithmic solutions described in the book can be integrated in commercial applications, thus augmenting the power of current animation and capturing tools.

Index

Cognitive Systems Monographs

Edited by R. Dillmann, Y. Nakamura, S. Schaal and D. Vernon

Vol. 1: Arena, P.; Patanè, L. (Eds.)
Spatial Temporal Patterns for
Action-Oriented Perception
in Roving Robots
425 p. 2009 [978-3-540-88463-7]

Vol. 2: Ivancevic, T.T.; Jovanovic, B.;
Djukic, S.; Djukic, M.; Markovic, S.
Complex Sports Biodynamics
326 p. 2009 [978-3-540-89970-9]

Vol. 3: Magnani, L.
Abductive Cognition
534 p. 2009 [978-3-642-03630-9]

Vol. 4: Azad, P.
Visual Perception for Manipulation
and Imitation in Humanoid Robots
270 p. 2009 [978-3-642-04228-7]

Vol. 5: de Aguiar, E.
Animation and Performance Capture
Using Digitized Models
168 p. 2010 [978-3-642-10315-5]